HENRY REYNOLDS

Mythomystes
[1632]

Introductory Note by
Arthur F. Kinney

Scolar Press
1972

SBN 85417 854 6

C

Printed in Great Britain by
The Scolar Press Limited
Menston, Yorkshire, England

NOTE

Mythomystes by H. R. (STC 20939) was so little recognized in its own time—I have been unable to trace a single contemporary reference to this singularly fascinating work—that we are left today to conjecture about its title, its author, and its date of publication. Although the OED does not give us a definition of the title of this work, clearly the author, who argues for the fourfold interpretation of texts now best defined for us in Dante's letter to Can Grande della Scala, intends to obscure the essential truth of his essay in the title itself. Appropriate to the age of metaphysical poetry as well as to the Neoplatonic poetic argued in this work, the title is a conceit of multiple meaning: *myth* refers both to the story or fable of a poetic work and to the parable which attempts to verbalize it, while *mystes* (i.e., plural of *mist*) entertains both the meanings of 'obscure', 'hidden,' and 'mystical,' 'spiritual'. Moreover, the compounding of both words leads us in the direction H. R. wishes to go: from the fable to the spiritual, from the fiction to what he terms the *most high Mysteries* (D4r) which poetry should convey.

The author was first identified as Michael Drayton's friend Henry Reynolds by John Payne Collier (*Bibliographical Account &c.*, I, 533); and, in this instance, at least, there seems little reason to dispute him. For H. R. presents here a roll call of English poets similar—and in the case of Daniel identical—to a longer roll call given us by Drayton in a poem entitled 'To my most dearely-loued friend HENERY REYNOLDS Esquire, of *Poets & Poesie*' published as part of *Elegies vpon Sundry Occasions* (1627). Indeed, in this poem Drayton gives us a charming picture of the two men contented with their literary conversation:

> My dearely loued friend how oft haue we,
> In winter evenings (meaning to be free,)
> To some well-chosen place vs'd to retire;
> And there with moderate meate, and wine, and fire,
> Haue past the howres contentedly with chat,
> Now talk of this, and then discours'd of that,
> Spoke our owne verses 'twixt our selues, if not
> Other mens lines, which we by chance had got,
> Or some Stage pieces famous long before,
> Of which your happy memory had store;
> And I remember you much pleased were,
> Of those who liued long agoe to heare,
> As well as of those, of these latter times,
> Who have inricht our language with their rimes,
> And in succession, how still vp they grew,
> Which is the subiect, that I now pursue.

(lines 1-16; ed. Cyril Brett [Clarendon, 1907], p. 108)

Drayton's poem also contains other scraps of evidence; for example, he treats Musaeus, Hesiod, and Homer (line 144) as H. R. does here (H2r). In addition, the 'TALE OF NARCISSVS' which is appended here (M3r-P1r) and which H. R. tells us he 'had diverse yeares since, put into English' (M3v) resembles rather closely Reynolds' *Torquato Tasso's Aminta Englisht* (London, 1628). Yet beyond this, we know precious little about Reynolds: only that he 'imitated' Anguillara's Ovid, and that nine poems are set to music in the books of Henry Lawes' *Ayres and Dialogues* (1653, 1655, 1658).

Mythomystes is undated, but we can learn the approximate date of its printing from the entry for the pamphlet in the Stationers' Register:

> Master John
> Waterson
>
> Entred for his Copy vnder the handes of Master BUCKNER and master Aspley warden a booke called *Mithomystes a Survey of Poetry* by HENRY REYNOLDS gent[leman]
>
> . . . . vjd
>
> (*SR*, ed. Arber, IV, 282)

The entry, made for 10 August 1632, is lined out, presumably by Waterson, 'by his owne Consent,' and the rights resigned to Reynolds '*vt patet supra &c.*' Gathering what data we can, then, it appears that *Mythomystes* is a Neoplatonic theory of literature by the translator Henry Reynolds which appeared briefly in a single edition in London in late 1632.

ii

Now, more than 400 years after the Platonic academy flowered in Florence, producing in Pico della Mirandola the seminal influence on Reynolds' poetics, what are we to make of this unique work, drawing syncretically, as Pico himself did, on pagan myth, Christian Scripture, and the cabala? Douglas Bush, no doubt annoyed by Reynolds' retreat to an arcane interest in Orpheus and Zoroaster, dismisses him abruptly as 'the exponent . . . of the allegorical-mystical theory of poetry' (*English Literature in the Earlier Seventeenth Century* [Oxford, 1945], p. 351). J. E. Spingarn is more extreme—and at greater length:

> In this perverse work, Henry Reynolds, the friend of Drayton and the translator of the *Aminta*, has given us the chief example in English of the systematic application of Neoplatonism to the interpretation of poetry. Bacon had already indicated the road, but Reynolds follows it into a tropical forest of strange fancies: the Cabalists and Neoplatonists, Philo and Reuchlin, but especially Pico della Mirandola and Alessandro Farra, here find an English voice.

Drayton's praise of his friend is justified by the wide culture which this book indicates, and the opening pages make one regret that its author has gone off at a tangent. (*Critical Essays of the Seventeenth Century* [Oxford, 1957], I, xxi)

Striving, however, to find some justification for a misuse of learning, Spingarn makes an interesting connection which soon becomes an overstatement:

> [Reynolds] belongs to the 'metaphysical school' of literary criticism; in this field the *Mythomystes* furnishes perhaps the only analogue of a method and state of mind illustrated in poetry by Donne and his epigones, in philosophy by the Cambridge Platonists, and in pulpit oratory by such men as Corbet and King. (I, xxi-xxii)

Spingarn's *aperçu* in thus linking Reynolds with the metaphysical poets —although Vaughan and Traherne, and perhaps Herbert, would have been better analogues than Donne—points to the interest all of them shared in suggesting important but ineffable truths by means of a language which was, by its very nature, inadequate for such a task. But, as Spingarn was himself aware, the use of symbol and metaphor—what Reynolds dismisses as 'tropes'—did not much concern the author of *Mythomystes*; even less was he attracted by the wit of paradox and oxymoron, those conceits of language by which 'The most heterogeneous ideas are yoked by violence together' that so annoyed Dr. Johnson.

We can locate Reynolds' contribution to critical thought pretty clearly, however, by looking at the contexts within which he wrote, and by noting what he chose to incorporate and what he ignored in fashioning his poetics. Ben Jonson's *Timber: or, Discoveries* (? c. 1612) conflated the three schools of thought emphasized by English critics throughout the sixteenth century, but most successfully synthesized by Sidney: from Plato, the idea that the poet was divinely inspired to create a comprehensible world not unlike Paradise; from Horace, the understanding that poetry should teach through delight (making Horace's twin ends of art a single means and end); from Aristotle, the technique of imitating a brazen world (mimesis) in order to sketch out an apprehensible golden world. Of these three main defenses of poetry, Reynolds emphasizes the first, subordinates the second, and ignores the third. About a fourth, lesser defense of poetry—the use of rhetoric as a basis for art which Hobbes in *Human Nature* (1650) would call 'those grateful similes, metaphors, and other tropes, by which both *poets* and *orators* have it in their power to make things please or displease, and shew well or ill to others, as they like themselves'—Reynolds is both explicit and negative: in calling for 'the reall Forme and Essence' of poetry (A3r-A3v), he rejects as distracting accidents (unnecessaries)

> *those floures (as they are called) of Rhetorick, consisting of . . .* Anaphoras, Epistrophes, Metaphors, Metonymyes, Synedoches *and those their other potent Tropes and Figures; helpes, (if at all of vse to furnish out expressions with,) much properer sure, and more fitly belonging to Poesy then Oratory; yet such helpes, as if Nature haue not beforehand in his byrth, giuen a Poet, all such forced Art will come behind as lame to the businesse, and deficient, as the best-taught countrey Morris dauncer with all his bells and napkins, will ill deserue to be in an Inne of Courte at Christmas, tearmed the thing they call a fine reueller.* (A3v)

This passage represents Reynolds at his most jocular, but such light-heartedness serves to underscore the little concern he has with such figures and tropes as Renaissance English poets and critics, from Elyot onward, were borrowing from the classical and medieval rhetoricians.

In choosing to ignore so many critical commonplaces, Reynolds, after Pico, chose to value the fables of poets not for their literal meaning (the narrative line) or their allegorical meaning (the moral lesson) or even for their moral meaning (as indicators of proper behaviour and models of emulative action), but chose instead to emphasize the anagogic meaning (or what the English Renaissance termed 'natural Philosophy,' perhaps to avoid the Dantean term which smacked to them of popery). This may not be surprising, if we consider that Reynolds' close friend Drayton, in turning the Ovidian myth of Endymion and Phoebe into a scientific lecture of sorts, had sought to focus on numerology and astrology; but for Reynolds such a remarking on the transcending and intellectual powers of poetic statement allowed him to concentrate on the poet's sensitivity, intuition and genius—the creative talents we label simply 'inspiration'—which the poetics of a Ben Jonson or a William Drummond of Hawthornden could not accommodate. ('What is not like the Ancients and conform to those Rules which hath been agreed vnto by all Times, may (indeed) be something like unto *Poesy*, but it is no more *Poesy* than a Monster is a Man,' Drummond wrote to Dr. Arthur Johnson, the King's physician, about 1629.) Long ago Cicero had accused Socrates of separating the tongue from the mind, a sentiment echoed in the sixteenth century by Roger Ascham: 'Ye know not, what hurt ye do to learning that care not for Words, but for Matter, and so make a Divorce betwixt the Tongue and the Heart.' No matter how hermetic Reynolds' poetics may seem, he is at least struggling to coalesce the human act of poetry with certain apprehended but transcendent truths which provide for him its only worthwhile matter.

Thus in many ways, Reynolds' position is extremely close to Sidney's. We might even argue, in fact, that it becomes before its end the cabalistic counterpart to Sidney's Neoplatonic theories. But Reynolds had a much more difficult time proving the value of his poetics than did his predecessor. His arcane interests aside, Reynolds had to oppose two other popular sentiments in his day. The first, that of the poetasters and their increasing audiences, was later delineated by Locke in *An Essay Concerning Humane Understanding* (1690): 'Men who have a great deal of Wit, . . . make vp pleasant Pictures, and agreeable Visions in Fancy . . . and therefore [their work] is so acceptable to all People, because [its] Beauty appears at first sight, and there is required no labor of thought, to examine what Truth and Reason there is in it. The Mind, without looking any further, rests satisfied with the agreeableness of the Picture, and the gayety of the Fancy.' Unlike Sidney, who theorized in manuscript for his courtly companions, Reynolds apparently chose to publish a poetics in an age of growing journalism and popular art. To add to his difficulty, he wished to pursue, as Plato had, the importance of poetic vision in the Age of Jonson dominated by neoclassical rules, first borrowed from Italy but made tantamount to a requirement in England. It is no wonder that Reynolds' work was issued in only one edition and was never mentioned by his contemporaries. The wonder is that he decided to publish it at all.

iii

Reynolds sets forth in his preface his purpose, to define 'the Essentiall Forme, of true Poesy' (A3r). The need is underscored by his regressive theory of history (B1r-B1v), a notion he shares with Gosson and Sidney as well as with Jonson: 'Wee liue in a myste, blind and benighted; and since our first fathers disobedience poysoned himselfe and his posterity, Man is become the imperfectest and most deficient Animall of all the field: for then he lost that Instinct that the Beast retaines; though with him the beast, and with it the whole vegitable and generall Terrene nature also suffered, and still groanes vnder the losse of their first purity, occasioned by his fall.' (G3v) (Even Jonson, in *Timber*, admitted that 'things daily fall, wits grow downward, and eloquence grows backward.') Hence, after an *exordium* which is given over to complaint rather than pleasant anecdote (in accord with Reynolds' distrust of the pleasant 'husk' given poetry), this *propositio*: by 'look[ing] backe to the neuer-enough honoured Auncients,' (C3v) Reynolds finds 'pleasing and profitable fictions . . . (The very fittest conduit-pipes) [which] deriue downe to vs the vnderstanding of things euen farthest remooued from vs, and most worthy our speculation, and knowledge.' (C1v) Entering the by-now familiar battle of the Ancients vs. the Moderns on the side of the former must have struck Reynolds' readers as reactionary, and he does modify his position with an abbreviated roll call of deservedly famous English poets from Chaucer to Daniel and Drayton himself (B4v-C1r), but such a position allows him to draw on Pico's list of cabalistic writers which, until Reynolds' time, no theorist of the English Renaissance had thought to bring so seriously to the defense of poetry. In the three major sub-divisions of his *affirmatio*, Reynolds turns repeatedly to this fresh evidence in support of the divine *afflatus* which he finds available only in the best poetry.

Reynolds notes that Plato called poets the Sons of God in *Republic II* and poetry's admission to understanding divine or intellectual love is Reynolds' first argument in favor of the unique (if to his audience, arcane) characteristics available to poetry.

> Rationall and wise Spirits are forcibly raised and lifted aloft; yea lifted oftentimes so far (sayes *Plato*) aboue mortality, as euen—*in Deum transeunt*, and so full fraught with the delight and abondance of the pleasure they feele in those their elevations, raptures, and mentall aliena-tions (wherin the soule remaines for a time quite seperated as it were from the body) do not only sing with the ingenious *Ouid: Est Deus in nobis, agitante calescimus illo*, [the quotation is from *Fasti* 6.5] But in an Extaticke manner, and to vse *Plato's* phrase [in the *Ion*] *diuino afflatu concitati*, cry out with the intraunced *Zoroaster-Ope thine eyes, ope them wide; raise and lift them aloft.* (C4v-D1r)

In citing Plato, and alluding here and elsewhere to remarks in the *Republic*, *Ion* and *Phaedrus*, Reynolds may also intend to suggest Plato's constant returning to inspired fictions, to divine messengers such as Diotima, and to divine visions such as the one which closes the *Republic*. Such divine intuition, Reynolds argues, makes poets into Tiereseas, so dazzled by their visions of the divine that they are blind to the mundane and earthbound. So acute are such visions that poets alone see the order in such transcendent systems of meaning as the doctrine of numbers. Yet one need not go quite so far as mystical numerology, for 'These were those fathers (as I lately called them) and fountes of knowledge and learning; or nurses of wisdome, from whose pregnant brests the whole world hath suckt the best part of all the humane knowledge it [i.e., that] it hath.' (D2v)

The second part of Reynolds' argument is a corollary to the first. Unlike modern writers, the ancients took care to preserve their know-ledge by concealing it from the vulgar; 'high and Mysticall matters should by riddles and enigmaticall knotts be kept inuiolate from the prophane Multitude.' (E3r-E3v) The greatest poets thus communicated only to an exclusive few; so Reynolds explains the hidden meanings in Orpheus' hymns and (quoting Pico) in the words of Orpheus' Christian counterpart, Moses. '*Moses* receiued from God vpon the mount not the Law only, which he hath left in fiue bookes exactly deliuered to posterity, but the more hidden also, and true explanation of the Law . . . those secreter Mysteries, and abstrusities of most high diuinity, hidden and concealed vnder the barke, and rude couer of the words, to haue diuulged and layd these open to the vulgar; what had it been other than to giue holy things to dogs, and cast pearles among swine?' (G1r-G1v) His third point is the obverse of this; that the uninitiated, in their ignorance, have no grounds to criticize such secret and inspired understanding.

It is in this final section of the *confirmatio* that Reynolds' own argument coincides most closely with Pico's. For Reynolds becomes syncretic, too: 'And beginning with *Moses*, shew them, all those—*dij maiorum gentium* from *Saturne* to *Deucalions* deluge, were but names for *Adam*, *Caine*, *Lamech* and the rest of their successors to *Noahs* floud: Nor that their *Rhaea* (or *Terra*, mother of all the Gods) and *Venus*, could be other then *Moses* his *Eua* and *Noema*. What other can *Hesiod's Pandora*—*the first and beautifullest of all women, by whome all euils were dispersed and spred vpon the Earth*, meane then *Moses* his *Eue*?' (L1v) Clearly Reynolds' assumption here, one which he shared with other seventeenth-century critics but not to such a degree as he pursued it, is that the most helpful and truthful poetics is that which accounts for the most evidence. That had also been Pico's position, to assimilate both Western and Eastern thought, pagan and sacred, classical and cabalistic.

What, in addition, makes Reynolds' poetics unique in this period of English literature is that he joins here the theoretical criticism with applied, or practical, criticism: he appends his own earlier translation of a poem, not directly from Ovid as he claims, but a paraphrase of Anguillara. In this story of Narcissus's 'tirannizing Passion' (O1v), Reynolds supplies a representative fable for man 'in his search of humane knowledge' (M3v); in his 'Obseruation' on the tale which follows his translation (P1r-P4r), he analyzes the poem by the fourfold method of interpretation so adored by the medieval preacher—here called 'the Geographick sense,' 'the Physick sense,' 'the Morall sence,' and, what is truly important, 'the Diuine sence.' Pico's illustrations, drawn often from Moses and Esdras, never themselves depended on his own artistic, but merely his philosophizing, efforts. By thus supplementing and concluding the arguments Pico set out in his *Oration* (and presumably, his 900 theses), Reynolds is justifiably his greatest English disciple in critical and poetical theory.

Reynolds concludes his main argument with an attack on Bacon whom he identifies only indirectly, by alluding to his *De Sapientia Veterum* (1609) and his *Advancement of Learning* (1605). In some ways, Reynolds is only shadow-boxing. No doubt he was angered by Bacon's statement that, in many the like encounters, I do rather think that the fable was first, and the exposition devised, than that the moral was first, and thereupon the fable framed.

(*Advancement*, 2.4)

But it was Bacon who also remarked that the fables were more antique than the poets who framed them and that many should be regarded

> not as the product of the age, or invention of the poets, but as sacred relics, gentle whispers, and the breath of better times, that from the traditions of more ancient nations came, at length, into the flutes and trumpets of the Greeks.

(*De Sapientia Veterum*, Preface)

Surely Bacon would not—and did not here—go so far as Reynolds would have him, but the very fact that the seventeenth-century champion of logic and reason was able to state even this shows that, aside from his intellectual companionship with Drayton, Reynolds was not altogether alien to his time. Indeed, there were others including the Cambridge Platonists: Alexander Ross, with his *Mel Heliconium* and *Mystagogus Poeticus* and Henry More with his *Conjectura Cabbalistica* and his *Defence of the Threefold Cabbala*, later ridiculed in *Spectator* no. 221. Of them all, Reynolds was surely the best, as he was the most devoted, English disciple of Pico, the last vestige in England of the Florentine Academy of the fifteenth century.

iv

The copy of *Mythomystes* used for the present facsimile is that in the Bodleian Library, bearing the shelfmark Arch A f 109. The copy which I have examined is that in the Houghton Library of Harvard University, with the shelfmark STC 20939. Both appear to be identical, having sig. C2 erroneously marked CC and sig. E2 reading F2. The Houghton copy is side-stitched; A1 and P4 serve as covers. The copy collates 4°; A-P4.

Reynolds' pamphlet was printed by Henry Seile, a London bookseller whose bookstall was first at the Tiger's Head in St. Paul's (from 1622 to 1636), then later moved to the sign of the Tiger's Head in Fleet Street, over against St. Dunstan's Church. Seile had taken up his freedom in 1619 (Arber, III, 654); he served as Master of the Stationers' Company in 1657. He died about 1661, the business passing on to one Anna Seile, presumably his widow.

Mythomystes was dedicated to the Right Honorable Lord, Henry, Lord Matravers, misidentified as Ma[l]travers in every commentary since Hazlitt. He is properly Henry Frederick (Howard), earl of Arundel, born

15 August 1608, the first surviving son and heir, who together with his eldest brother was created a Knight Bachelor on 4 November 1616. Like several of his predecessors since the earlier sixteenth century, Henry arbitrarily assumed the title of Lord Mautravers, from an ancestor who had married into the Arundel family in 1377, taking up the Arundel line as barony of writ. Lord Henry served as a member of Parliament for Arundel in 1628/9 and in 1640 and for Callan, Ireland, in 1634. He was later an ardent Royalist who was present at the battle of Edgehill. Perhaps the most interesting fact concerning Reynolds' presumed patron is Lord Henry's marriage, on 7 March 1625/6, to Elizabeth, the daughter of Esme (Stuart), third duke of Lennox. Lord Henry died, aged 44, on 17 April 1652, and was buried at Arundel.

It may be assured *Mythomystes* had but one edition; presumably an edition of 1643, mentioned by Hazlitt (*Handbook to the Popular Poetical and Dramatic Literature of Great Britain* [London, 1867], p. 502), is a ghost. Lowndes (*Bibliographer's Manual of English Literature* [London, 1857], p. 2031) and Collier knew of only one edition. The date of 1632, ascertained through the Stationers' Register, is verified by internal evidence: Reynolds speaks of Drayton's 'late-writ' *Agincourt* (C1), published in 1627, and speaks of Chapman, who died in 1634, as still living—'one (and the best) of our Greeke translators' (H2r). *Mythomystes* is now exceedingly rare; in the eighteenth century, a copy was valued at £1 12s.; in the 1933 Britwell handlist of the Britwell Court Collection in Buckinghamshire, Quaritch lists a copy selling for £240. The pamphlet was not reprinted until modern times, but there have been two modern editions of Reynolds' main text both in slightly modernized spelling and annotated: J. E. Spingarn, *Critical Essays of the Seventeenth Century* (Oxford, 1908; 1957), I, 141-179; and Edward W. Tayler, ed., *Literary Criticism of Seventeenth-Century England* (New York, 1967), 225-258.

Both these editions omit 'THE TALE OF NARCISSVS briefly Mythologized,' but it has had two editions of its own in this century. The poem, which Bush has called 'quite successful' in its translation of the 'liquid movement' of the Italian (*Mythology and the Renaissance Tradition in English Poetry*, rev. ed. [New York, 1963], p. 334) was first reprinted in *Englische Studien*, 35 (1905), 260 ff. and, in the following year, as Extra Series no.3 in the Orinda Booklets (Hull, 1906).

ARTHUR F. KINNEY

University of Massachusetts (Amherst), USA

Following are literal translations of foreign phrases in Reynolds' text. Passages not included here are translated by Reynolds himself in the body of the work.

B3r	*Decipiantur in nomine diaboli*	Let them be deceived in the name of the devil
C2v	*Non quia Graeca scias, . . . sed quia vera vides*	You are not learned or wise because you may be well-versed in Greek and in Latin but because you perceive truth
C3r	*tanquam parui pueri . . . sunt solliciti.*	As little boys loiter by the fire through the winter, old women drink in the trifles and fables of poets [i.e., old wives' tales], though in the meanwhile they remain not in the least aroused with more useful, more holy, thought.
C4v	*in Deum transeunt*	They pass into God
C4v	*Est Deus in nobis, agitante calescimus illo*	A God is in us, we grow heated to the extent that he moves us
D1r	*diuino afflatu concitati*	quickened with divine afflatus
D3r	*Orpheus apud Graecos . . . patres & authores.*	The virtually complete Orpheus was read among the Greeks; Zoroaster is known only imperfectly, though among the Chaldeans he is read in a more complete text. Both (*sayes he*) are fathers and authors of ancient wisdom.
D3v	*Sapientiae patres, ac duces*	The fathers of wisdom and even the guides
E1r	*Qual vaghezza di lauro, . . . guadagno intesa.*	Is the love of laurel and myrtle gone? You go naked and poor, philosophy. The crowd, bent on vile lucre, has its say.
E1v-E2r	*pudicam Palladem, . . . in amatoris arculam referat.*	Chaste Pallas, sent among the diverse mass of men as the gift of the gods, is thrown aside, hooted out, and hissed; not having anyone who loves her, who cherishes her, unless by prostituting herself, as it were, she puts the poor rewards, accepted as the price of tarnished virginity, in with the small change of her lover.
E2v	*non concessum*	nonconcession
E2v	*comiter erranti monstrare viam.*	courteously pointed out the way to one who has strayed.
E3v	*priscae sapientiae patres*	fathers of ancient wisdom
E3v	*Secreta de numeris doctrina*	arcane doctrine of numbers
E3v	*Magnum & sublime*	great and sublime
E3v	*ut a primo fonte manare*	as from the original fountain flow
E4r	*Omnia in his, & ab his sunt omnia.*	All things are in these, and from these all things are.
E4v	*editi, & non editi*	written, & not written
G2r	*Sanctum . . . margaritas.*	holy things to dogs, and cast pearls among swine (as earlier).
G4r	*In quella . . . s'asconde*	In that inaccessible light, as if in an exalted fog it hides itself
H3v	*Scala a Tartaro ad primum ignem*	A ladder from Tartarus to the first fire
I1r	*Orpheus . . . excogitauit, &c.*	Orpheus found many things useful to human and political life, and he was the first who unfolded all theology and devised atonements for nefarious crimes.

I4r	*Sustentacula vitae*	The supports of life
K4r	*(fecisti nos Domine propter te*	you made us, Lord, near to yourself
L1v	*dij maiorum gentium*	The gods of the greater nations
L2r	*Nulli subigebant . . . ferebat;*	No farmers subjugated the soil . . . . And the earth brought forth more freely of herself when no one begged.
L2v	*Luctus, . . . & turpis egestas.*	Grief and vengeful cares have made their bed; there live pale diseases and sorrowful old age, and fear, and hunger the cause of evil, and vile want.
L2v	*Locus amaenissimus, & voluptatis plenissimus*	A most pleasing place, and most full of delights
L4v	*Veritas . . . praeualebit:*	Truth is great and will prevail.
M1r	*Vilia miretur vulgus*	Let the vulgar crowd esteem the tawdry
M1r	*Simile habent sua labra lactucas*	like lips, like lettuce, [i.e., like meets like]

MYTHOMYSTES

WHEREIN

A SHORT SVRVAY

IS TAKEN OF THE

NATVRE AND VALVE

OF TRVE POESY, AND

DEPTH OF THE ANCIENTS

ABOVE OVR MODERNE

POETS.

*To which is annexed the Tale
of Narcissus briefly
mythologized*

LONDON,
Printed for *Henry Seyle*, at the Tigers-head
in S^t. *Pauls* Church-yard.

To the *Right Hon*ll: *and my*
euer-honor'd Lord,
Henry Lord Matrauers.

M Y   L O R D

As I haue euer
beene a louer
(*though ignorant one*) *of the*
Art of Painting, a frute of the
Fancy that may be fitly called a
filent Poëfy , fo of necefsity muft
I loue her Sifter the Art of Poë-
fy,which is no other then a fpeak-
ing Painting or Picture.And be-
*caufe I prefume your Lo*p: *fauo-*
ring, and fo well vnderftanding
the one , cannot but vnderftand,
and like the other, I aduenture to
prefent a flight drafte of her to
*your Lo*p: *that as you haue daily*

A 2   *before*

before your eyes, one of the best
suruayes of what is, or can be in
Picture, you may haue likewise
limned, though in little, by a
creature no lesse your owne then
they are (how artfully I dare not
auouch, but sure) a true picture of
her Sister Poësy. A Birth (my
Lord) some moneths since conceiued, and euen as soone borne;
and which, though now ope to o-
ther eyes, yet askes no other honour then your acceptance; to
whome in gratefull acknowledg-
ment of your noble fauours, are
(no lesse then this his slight issue
is,) for euer dedicated the best of
the poore indeauors of the pa-
rent

Your Lop. humble, and most
affectionate seruant

H: R:

TO THE CANDID AND INGENVOVS READER.

LOoke not generous Reader (for such I write to) for more in the few following leaues, then a plaine and simple verity; vnadorned at all with eloquution, or Rhetoricall phrase; glosses fitter perhaps to be set vpon silken and thinne paradoxicall semblances, then appertaining to the care of who desires to lay downe a naked & vnmasked Trueth. Nor expect heere an Encomium or praise of any such thing as the world ordinarily takes Poësy for; That same thing beeing (as I conceiue) a superficiall meere outside of Sence, or gaye barke only (without the body) of Reason; witnesse so many excellent witts that haue taken so much paines in these times to defend her; which sure they would not haue done, if what is generally receiued now a dayes for Poësy, were not meerely a faculty, or occupation of so little consequence, as by the louers thereof rather to be (in their owne fauour) excused, then for any good in the thing it selfe, to be commended. Nor must thou heere expect thy solution, if thy curiosity inuite thee to a satisfaction in any the vnder-Accidents, but in meerely the Essentiall Forme, of true Poësy: Such I call the Accidents or appendixes thereto, as conduce somewhat to the Matter, aud End, nothing to the reall Forme
and

and *Eſſence thereof.* *And theſe accidents (as I call them) our commenders & defenders of Poëſy haue chiefely, and indeed ſufficiently inſiſted, and dilated vpon ; and are firſt , thoſe floures (as they are called) of Rhetorick, conſiſting of their* Anaphoras, Epiſtrophes , Metaphors, Metonymyes, Synecdoches *and thoſe their other potent Tropes and Figures; helpes, (if at all of vſe to furniſh out expreſſions with,) much properer ſure , and more fitly belonging to Poëſy then Oratory ; yet ſuch helpes , as if Nature haue not beforehand in his byrth, giuen a Poët, all ſuch forced Art will come behind as lame to the buſineſſe, and deficient , as the beſt-taught countrey Morris dauncer with all his bells and napkins, will ill deſerue to be in an Inne of Courte at Chriſtmas , tearmed the thing they call a fine reueller. The other Accidents of Poëſy, and that are the greater part of the appurtenances thereof, in the accoumpt of our Poëts of theſe times, are alſo heere vtterly vnmencioned ; ſuch as are , what ſort of Poëme may admit the blanke verſe, what requires exacte rime ; where the ſtrong line (as they call it) where the gentle , ſortes beſt ; what ſubject muſt haue the verſe of ſo many feete , what of other ; where the maſculine rime , where the feminine , and where the threeſillabled (which the Italians call their* rime ſdrucciole) *are to be vſed. Theſe (I ſay) and the like Adjuncts of Poëſy, (elſewhere amply diſcourſed of by many curious witts) are*

not

not heere mencioned. Only what I conceiued fit to speake (and with what breuity I could) of the Auncient Poëts in generall, and of the Forme and reall Essence of true Poësy, considered meerely in it owne worth and validity, without extrinsick and suppeditatiue ornament at all, together with the paralell of their foyle (our Moderne Poëts and Poësyes,) I haue, (to the end to redeeme in some parte, and vindicate that excellent Art from the iniury it suffers in the worlds generall misprizion and misconstruction thereof,) heere touched, and but touched; the rather to awake some abler vnderstanding then my owne, to the pursute (if they please) of a theame (I conceiue) well worthy a greater industry, and happyer leisures then I my selfe possesse.

MYTHO-

MYTHOMYSTES.

WHEREIN A SHORT SVRVAY IS TAKEN OF THE NATVRE AND VALVE OF TRVE Poëſie, and depth of the Ancients aboue our Moderne Poëts.

 Haue thought vpon the times wee liue in ; and am forced to affirme the world is decrepit , and out of its age & doating eſtate,ſubieĉt to all the imperfeĉtions that are inſeparable from that wracke and maime of Nature,that the young behold with horror, and the ſufferers thereof lye vnder with murmur and languiſhmēt.Euen the generall Soule of this great Creature , whereof eue-

ry one of ours is a ſeuerall peece,
ſeemes bedrid, as vpon her deathbed,
and neere the time of her diſſolution
to a ſecond better eſtate, and being:
the yeares of her ſtrength are paſt;
and ſhe is now nothing but diſeaſe
for the Soules health is no other than
meerely the knowledge of the Truth
of things. Which health, the worlds
youth inioyed; and hath now * ex-
changed for it, all the diſeaſes of
all errors, hereſies, and different
ſects and ſchiſmes of opinions and vn-
derſtandings in all matter of Arts,
Sciences, and Learnings whatſoeuer.
To helpe on theſe diſeaſes to incura-
bility, what age hath euer beene ſo
fruitfull of liberty in all kindes, and of
all permiſſion and allowance for this
reaſon of ours, to runne wildely all
her owne hurtfulleſt wayes without
bridle, bound, or limit at all? For inſtance; what bookes haue wee of
what

* For the
world hath
loſt his youth,
and the times
begin to waxe
old. 2 Eſd.
cap. 14.

what euer knowledge, or in what myfteries foeuer, wifely by our Auncients (for auoiding of this prefent malady the world is now falne into) couched, and carefully infoulded, but muft bee by euery illiterate perfon without exception, deflowred and broke open, or broke in pieces, becaufe beyond his skill to vnlocke thé? Or what Law haue we that prouides for the reftraint of thefe myriads of hotheaded wranglers, &ignorant writers and teachers, which, out of the bare priuiledge of perhaps but puny graduate in fome Vniuerfity, will venter vpon all, euen the moft remoued and moft abftrufe knowledges, as perfect vnderftanders and expounders of them, vpon the fingle warrant of their owne braine; or inuenters of better themfelues, than all Antiquity could deliuer downe to them ; out of the treafonous mint of their owne i-

B 2   maginations?

maginations? What hauocke, what
mifchiefe to all learnings, and how
great a multiplicity of poyfonous
errours and herefies muft not of
neceffity hence enfue, and ouer-
fpread the face of all Truths whatfo-
euer?

Among thefe herefies (to omit
thofe in matter of Diuinity, or the
right forme of worfhipping God,
which the Doctors of his Church are
fitter to make the fubiects of their
tongues and pens, than I, a Layman,
and all-vnworthy the taske,) among,
I fay, thefe, (if I may fo call them)
herefies, or ridiculous abfurdities in
matter of humane letters, and their
profeffors in thefe times, I find none
fo groffe, nor indeed any fo great fcan-
dall, or maime to humane learning, as
in the almoft generall abufe, and violence offered to the excellent art of
Poefye; firft, by thofe learned (as they
thinke

thinke themfelues) of our dayes, who call themfelues Poets ; and next , by fuch as out of their ignorance, heede not how much they prophane that high and facred title in calling them fo.

From the number of thefe firft mentioned,(for,for the laft, I will not mention them ; nor yet fay as a graue Father, and holy one too , of certaine obftinate heretikes faid ; *Decipiantur in nomine diaboli* ; but charitably wifh their reformaticn, and cure of their blindneffe ;) from the multitude (I fay) of the common rimers in thefe our moderne times , and moderne tongues , I will exempt fome few , as of a better ranke and condition than the reft. And firft to beginne with *Spaine.* I will fay it may iuftly boaft to haue afforded (but many Ages fince) excellent Poets, as *Seneca,* the Trage-dian , *Lucan,* and *Martiall* the Epi-grammatift, with others ; and in thefe latter

latter times, as diuerfe in Profe, fome
good Theologians alfo in Rime; but
for other Poefies in their (now fpokē)
tongue, of any great name, (not to ex-
toll their trifling, though extolled
Celeftina, nor the fecond part of their
Diana de Monte Major, better much
than the firft; and thefe but poeticke
profers neither,)I cannot fay it affords
many, if any at all : The inclination
of that people being to fpend much
more wit, and more happily in thofe
profe *Romances* they abound in, fuch
as their *Lazarillo*, *Don Quixote*, *Guz-
man*, and thofe kind of *Cuenta's* of their
Picaro's, and *Gitanillas*, than in Rime.
The *French* likewife, more than for a
Ronfart, or *Des-Portes*, but chiefly
their *Saluft*, (who may paffe among
the beft of our modernes,) I can fay
little of. *Italy* hath in all times, as in
all abilities of the mind befides, been
much fertiler than either of thefe, in
Poets.

Poets. Among whom , (to omit a
Petrarch , who though he was an excellent rimer in his owne tongue , and
for his Latine *Africa* iuſtly deſerued
the lawrell that was giuen him ; yet
was a much excellenter Philoſopher
in profe ; and with him , a *Bembo* ,
Dante, Ang : *Politiano, Caporale, Pietro A-
retino* , *Sannazaro* , *Guarini* , and diuers
others, men of rare fancy all) I muſt
preferre chiefely three ; as the graue
and learned *Taſſo* , in his *ſette giorni*,
(a diuine worke) and his *Gieruſalem
liberata* , ſo farre as an excellent pile of
meerely Morall Philoſophy may deſerue. Then, *Arioſto* , for the artfull
woofe of his ingenious , though vn-
meaning fables ; the beſt , perhaps ,
haue in that kind beene ſung ſince
Ouid. And laſtly, that ſmoothwrit
Adonis of *Marino* , full of various con-
ception, and diuerſity of learning. The
Douche I cannot mention , being a
ſtranger

ftranger to their minds, and manners; therefore I will returne home to my Countrey-men, and mother tongue: And heere, exempt from the reſt, a *Chaucer*, for ſome of his poëms, chiefe-ly his *Troylus* and *Cresſide*. Then the generous and ingenious *Sidney*, for his ſmooth and artfull *Arcadia.* (and who I could wiſh had choze rather to haue left vs of his pen, an Encomiaſticke Poeme in honour, then proſe-Apo-logy in defence, of his fauorite, the excellent Art of Poeſy.) Next, I muſt approue the learned *Spencer*, in the reſt of his Poëms, no leſſe then his *Fairy Queene*, an exact body of the *Ethicke* doctrine : though ſome good iudgments haue wiſht (and perhaps not without cauſe) that he had there-in beene a little freer of his fiction, and not ſo cloſe riuetted to his Mo-rall; no leſſe then many doe to *Da-niells Ciuile warrs*, that it were (though

otherwiſe

otherwife a commendable worke)yet
fomwhat more than a true Chronicle
hiftory in rime; who, in other leffe
laboured things, may haue indeed
more happily, (how euer, alwayes
cleerely and fmoothly) written. Wee
haue among vs a late-writ *Polyolbion*
alfo, and an *Agincourte*, wherin I will
only blame their honeft Authours ill
fate, in not hauing laid him out fome
happier Clime, to haue giuen honour
and life to, in fome happier language.
After thefe, (befides fome late dead)
there are others now liuing, dramm-
maticke and liricke writers, that I
muft deferuedly commend for thofe
parts of fancy and imagination they
poffeffe; and fhould much more, could
wee fee them fomewhat more, force
thofe gifts, and liberall graces of Nature, to the end fhee gaue them; and
therewith, worke and conftantly tire
vpon follid knowledges; the which

C   hauing

hauing from the rich fountes of our
reuerend Auncients , drawne with
vnwearied , and wholfomely imploi-
ed induftries ; they might in no leſſe
pleaſing and profitable fictions than
they haue done (the very fitteſt conduit-pipes) deriue downe to vs the
vnderſtanding of things euen fartheſt
remooued from vs, and moſt worthy
our fpeculation, and knowledge. But
alas, ſuch children of obedience , I
muſt take leaue to ſay , the moſt of
our ordinary pretenders to Poeſy now
a dayes , are to their owne , and the
diſeaſed times ill habits, as the racke
will not bee able to make the moſt
aduiſed among twenty of them con-
feſſe , to haue farther inquired , or attended to more , in the beſt of their
Authours they haue choſen to read
and ſtudy , than meerely his ſtile,
phraſe , and manner of expreſſion ; or
ſcarce ſuffered themſelues to looke
beyond

beyond the dimenſion of their owne braine, for any better counſaile or inſtruction elſewhere. What can wee expect then of the Poems they write?, Or what can a man mee thinks liken them more fitly to, than to *Ixion's* iſſue ? for hee that with meerely a naturall veine, (and a little vanity of nature, which I can be content to allow a Poet) writes without other grounds of ſollid learning, than the beſt of theſe vngrounded rimers vnderſtád or aime at, what does he more than imbrace aſſembled cloudes with *Ixion,* and beget only Monſters? This might yet be borne with, did not theſe people as cófidently vſurpe to themſelues the title of *S*chollers, and learned men, as if they poſſeſt the knowledges of all the *Magi*, the wiſe Eaſt did euer breed; when, let me demand but a reaſon for ſecurity of my iudgement in allowing them for ſuch, they

C 2   ſtraite

ſtraite giue mee to know they vnder-
ſtand the *Greeke*, and *Latine*; and in
concluſion, I diſcouer, the compleate
crowne of all their ambition is but to
be ſtiled by others a good *Latiniſt* or
Grecian, and then they ſtile themſelues
good Schollers. So would I too, had I
not before hand beene taught to ſay :
*Non quia Græca ſcias, vel calles verba La-
tina, Doctus es aut ſapiens, ſed quia vera vi-
des*; & beſides, hapned to know a late
trauailing *Odcombian* among vs; that
became (I know not for what mortal-
ler ſinne than his variety of language)
the common ſcorne, and contempt of
all the abuſiue witts of the time; yet
poſſeſt both thoſe languages in great
perfection ; as his eloquent orations
in both toungs ; (and vttered vpon
his owne* head without prompting)
haue euer ſufficiently teſtified. Now,
finding this to be the greater part of
the Schollerſhip theſe our Poets in-

deauour

*For they
made him
ſtand, and
ſpeake
Greeke vpon
his head
with his
heeles vp-
ward.

deauour to haue, and which many of them alfo haue; I find with all, they fit downe as fatisfied, as if their vnfurnifht brefts contained each one the learning and wifdome of an *Orpheus*, *Virgil*, *Hefiod*, *Pindarus*, and *Homer* altogether. When as, what haue they elfe but the barke and cloathing meerely wherein their high and profound doctrines lay? Neuer looking farther into thofe their golden fictions for any higher fence, or any thing diuiner in them infoulded & hid from the vulgar, but lulled with the meruelleus exprefsion & artfull contexture of their fables-*tanquam parui pueri* (as one faies) *per brumam ad ignem fefsitantes, aniles nugas fabelláfque de Poëtis imbibunt, cum interim de vtiliore fanctioréque fententia minime funt folliciti.*

I haue ftaid longer, and rubde harder mee thinkes than needes, vpon the fore of our now a day Poets. Let mee
leaue

leaue them, and looke backe to the
neuer-enough honoured Auncients;
and fet them before our eyes, who no
leffe deferuedly wore the name of
Prophets, and Priuy-counfellors of
the Gods (to vfe their owne * phrafe,
or Sonnes of the Gods, as *Plato* * calls
them) than Poets. To the end wee
may, if in this declining ftate of the
world we cannot rectify our oblique
one, by their perfect and ftrait line,
yet indeauour it: and in the meane
time giue the awefull reuerence due
to them, for the many regions of di-
ftance between their knowledges and
ours. And this that wee may the
better doe, let vs paralell them with
the Poets (if I may fo call them) of
our times, in three things only, and
fo carry along together their ftrait
and our crooked line; for our better
knowledge of them, and reformation
of our felues. In the firft place then,
let

Hom. in
Odiff.
De Repub.
lib. 2.

let vs take a furuay of their naturall inclination and propenfeneffe to the acquifitió of the knowledge of truth, by what is deliuered to vs of them; as alfo, of their willing neglect, and a-uerfion from all worldiy bufineffe and cogitations that might be hindrances in the way to their defired end.

1. It is in humane experience found, as well as by all writers determined, that the powerfulleft of al the affects of the minde is Loue, and therefore the diuine *Plato** fayes,it is iuftly cal- * *In Phædro.* led *Roma* ; which among the Greeks, is force, potency, or vehemence. Of this Loue there be two kinds ; Cele-ftiall or Intellectuall; or elfe Carnall or Vulgar. Of both thefe kinds *Salomon* hath fpoken excellently ; of the Vul-gar, in his Prouerbes as a Morall, and in his Ecclefiaftes as a Naturall Phi-lofopher ; and diuine-like of the di-uine and Intellectuall Loue in his
Canticle;

Canticle ; for which it is called a-
mong all the reſt of the holy Scripture *Canticum canticorum* , as the moſt
ſacred and diuine. The obiect of this
Celeſtiall or Intellectuall Loue, (for
the other , or vulgar Loue it concernes mee not to mention,) is the
excellency of the Beauty of Supernall
and Intellectuall thinges : To the
contemplation whereof, rationall and
wiſe Spirits are forcibly raiſed and
lifted aloft ; yea lifted oftentimes ſo
far (ſayes *Plato*) * aboue mortality, as
euen-*in Deum tranſeunt* , and ſo full
fraught with the delight and abon-
dance of the pleaſure they feele in
thoſe their eleuations , raptures , and
mentall alienations (wherin the ſoule
remaines for a time quite ſeperated as
it were from the body) do not only
ſing with the ingenious *Ouid* ... *Eſt*
Deus in nobis, agitante caleſcimus illo, But
in an Extaticke manner, and to vſe
Plato's

* *In Ione.*

Plato's * phrafe) *diuino afflatu cōcitati,* cry   * *ʔn Iöne.*
out with the intraunced *Zoroafter-*
Ope thine eyes, ope them wide ; raife and
lift them aloft. And of this, the excellent Prince *Io: Picus-Mirandula,*
(in a difcourfe of his vpon the doctrine of *Plato*) giues the reafon; fay-
ing : *Such, whofe ʊnderftanding (being*
by Philofophicall ftudie refined and illumi-
nated) knowes this fenfible Beauty to bee
but the image of another more pure and
excellent, leauing the loue of this, defire to
fee the other ; and perfeuering in this ele-
uation of the minde, arriue at laft to that
celeftiall loue ; which although it liues in
the ʊnderftanding of the foule of euery
man, yet they only (fayes he) *make ʊfe*
of it, and they are but few, who feparating
themfelues wholy from the care of the bo-
dy, feeme thence oftentimes extaticke, and
as it were quite rauifht and exalted aboue
the earth and all earthly amufements. And
farther,in another place of that **Trea**- Fol. 507.
D   tife

tife , adds that many with the feruent
loue of the beauty and excellence
of intellectuall things , haue beene
fo raized aboue all earthly confidera-
tions,as they haue loft the vfe of their
corporall eyes. *Homer* (fayes he) *with*
feeing the ghoft of Achilles, which infpired
him with that Poeticke fury, that who with
vnderftanding reades , fhall find to con-
taine in it all intellectuall contemplation,was
thereby depriued (or faigned to bee depriued) *of his corporall eye-fight* , as one
that feeing all things aboue , could
not attend to the heeding of triuiall
and meaner things below. And fuch
rapture of the fpirit, is expreft (faies
he) *in the fable of Tyrefias that Calimacus*
fings ; who for hauing feene Pallas naked
(which fignifies no other than that Ideall
beauty,whence proceeds all fincere wifdome,
and not cloathed or couered with corporall
matter) became fodainly blind , and was by
the fame Pallas made a Prophet; *fo as that*
which

which blinded his corporall eyes, opened to him the eyes of his vnderstanding; by which he saw not only all things past, but also all that were to come.

Loe, these, and such Spirits as these the learned *Picus* speakes of , such were those of those Auncient Fathers of all learning , and *Tyresia*-like Prophets, as Poets : such their neglect of the body, and businesse of the world! Such their blindnesse to all things of triuiall and inferiour condition ; And such lastly were those extaticke eleuations; or that truly-*diuinus furor* of theirs, which *Plato* speaking of * sayes * In Ïöne. it is-*a thing so sacred , as-non sine maximo fauore Dei comparari queat ;* cannot bee attained to without the wonderfull fauour of God. And which selfe thing themselues ment in their fable of that beautifull *Ganimede*, they sing of , (which interpreted , is the Contemplation of the Soule , or the Ra-

tionall

tionall part of Man) fo deare to the
God of gods and men, as that he rai-
feth it vp to heauen , there to powre
out to him (as they make him his
cupbearer) the foueraigne Nectar of
Sapience and wifdome , the liquor he
is onely beft pleafed and delighted
with. Thefe were thofe fathers (as I
lately called them) and fountes of
knowledge and learning ; or nurfes of
wifdome, from whofe pregnant brefts
the whole world hath fuckt the beft
part of all the humane knowledge it
it hath ; And from whofe wife and
excellent fables (as * one of our late

Nata: Co-mes,

Mythologians truely notes) *All thofe
were after them called Philofophers* tooke
their grounds and firft *initia Philofo-
phandi* ; adding,that their Philofophy
was no other than meerely-*fabularum
fenfa ab inuolucris exuuijfque fabularum
explicata*-the fenfes and meanings of
fables taken out and feperated from
their

their huskes and inuoluements. With whom the excellent *Io: Picus* (or rather *Phænix* as wisemen * haue named him) consenting, sayes in his *Apologia* (speaking of the Poesies of *Zoroaster* and *Orpheus*)-*Orpheus apud Græcos fermè integer ; Zoroaster apud eos mancus, apud Caldæos absolutior legitur. Ambo* (sayes he) *priscæ Sapientiæ patres & authores.* Both of them fathers and authors of the auncient Wisdome. With these also the most autenticke *Iamblicus*, the *Caldean*, who writes-*Pythagoras* had-*Orphicam Theologiam tanquam exemplar, ad quam ipse suam effingeret formaretque philosophiam ;* the Theology of *Orpheus* as his coppy and patterne, by which hee formed and fashioned his philosophy. I will ad a word more of the before-cited *Picus*; who thus far farther of *Orpheus* in particular * sayes-*Secreta de Numeris doctrina, & quicquid magnum subli-meque*

* *Ang: Politianus,* (who likewise calls him-*Doctiorum omnium doctissimus,*) *Pau: Iouius, Biroaldus,* and our Sir *Tho: Moore,* who (among infinite many others) hath voluminously writ his praises.

* *In Apolog. fol.* 83.

*mèque habuit Græca philosophia, ab Or-
phei institutis vt a primo fonte manauit;*
the mysticall doctrine of Numbers,
and what euer the Greeke philosophy had in it great and high, flowed
all from the Institutions of *Orpheus,*
as from their first fount. And of the
rest of his ranke and fraternity, those-
Sapientiæ patres, ac duces (as *Plato* * calls
those old excellent Poets), I will
conclude in generall, with the testi-
mony of first, the now-mentioned
Plato; who sayes likewise elsewhere
* *Nihil aliud sunt quàm deorum inter-
pretes;* they are no other than the Interpreters of the gods. And in another
place * that-their *præclara poemata
non hominum sunt inuenta, sed cælestia
munera.* Their excellent Poëms are not
the inuentions of men, but gifts and
and graces of heauen. And lastly with
Farra the learned *Alexandrian,* who
speaking likewise * of the old Poets,
sayes-

*In Lyside.

*In Ione.

*In Phædro.

*In Settena.
Fol. 320.

fayes-*Their fables are all full of moſt high
Myſteries; and haue in them that ſplendor
that is ſhed into the fancy and intellect, ra-
uiſht, and inflamed with diuine fury.* And
in the ſameTreatiſe makes this parti- *fol.* 322.
cular mention of ſome of them-*and in
thoſe times flouriſhed Linus, Orpheus,Mu-
ſeus,Homer, Heſiod, and all the other moſt
famous of that truly golden age.*

Now to apply this ſhort view we
haue taken of theſe auncient Poets;
whither there appeares ought in any
our ſtudents, or writers of our times,
be they Poets or Philoſophers (I put
them together, as who are, or ſhould
be both profeſſors of but one, and the
ſame learning, though by the one receiued and deliuered in the apparell
of verſe, the other of proſe,) that may
in any degree of coherence ſuffer a
paralell with either the Inclinations
or Abilities of ſuch as theſe before
mentioned, I wiſh we could ſee cauſe
to

to grant. but rather, that there is in
them (for ought appeares) no such
inclination to the loue or search of a-
ny great or high truthes (for the
Truthes sake, meerely) nor the like
neglect of the world and blindnesse
to the vanities thereof, in respect of
it, nor lastly, any fruites from them,
sauouring of the like Industry, or bearing any shadow scarce of similitude
with that of theirs, wee may posi-
tiuely affirme; as a truth no lesse obuious to euery mans eye, than the la-
mentable cause and occasion thereof
is to euery mans vnderstading; which
is the meane accoumpt, or rather
contempt and scorne that in these
dayes, all vngaining Sciences, & that
conduce not immediately to worldly profit, or popular eminence, are
held in the Poet especially.

Qual

Qual vagbezza di lauro, qual di mirto?
Pouera, e nuda vai filofofia,
Dice la turba al vil guadagno intefa.

Whence it is, that much time fpent
in follid contemplatiue ftudies is held
vaine and vnneceffary; and thefe flight
flafhes of vngroūded fancy, (ingenious
Nothings, & meere imbroideries vpō
copwebbs) that the world fwarmes
with, (like fophifticate alchimy gold
that will not abide the firft touch, yet
glitters more in the eye than the fadd
weight yer true gold), are only laboured for and attended too; becaufe they
take beft, and moft pleafe the cor-
rupt taft and falfe appetite of the for-
did and barbarous times wee liue in.
And yet to fpeake a troth, I cannot
herein blame the difeafed world fo
much, as I do the infelicity of that facred Art of Poefy; which like the
foueraigne prefcriptions of a *Galen*
or *Hypocrates*, ordered and difpen-
E   fed

fed by illiterate Empyricks or dog-
leeches, muſt needes (as the beſt phi-
ſicks ill handled) proue but ſo much
variety of poyſon inſtead of cure. And
ſuch are the mont'ibanke Rimers of
the time, and ſo faulty, that haue ſo
much abuſed their profeſſion, and the
world; and ſtucke ſo generall a ſcan-
dall vpon that excellent Phyſicke of
the minde; with the poyſon of their
meritricious flatteries, and baſe ſer-
uile fawning at the heeles of worldly
wealth and greatneſle, as makes it
abhorred of all men ; and moſt, of
thoſe that are of moſt vnderſtanding.
For indeed what can bee more con-
temptible, or breed a greater indigna-
tion in wiſe, and vnderſtanding minds,
than to ſee the ſtudy of Wiſdome
made not only a mercinary, but viti-
ous occupation. And that ſame *pudicam Palladem*, (as a wiſe Author from
the like reſentment aptly ſaies) *deorum*
munere

munere inter homines diuersantem eijci, ex-
plodi, exibilari ; Non habere qui amet , qui
faueat , nisi ipsa quasi prostans , & præslo-
ratæ virginitatis accepta mercedula, male-
paratum æs in amatoris arculam refe-
rat.

   2. The second great difparity, that
I find betweene thofe auncient Fathers of learning , and our moderne
writers , is in the price and eftimati-
on they held their knowledges in.
Which appeares in the care they
tooke to conceale them from the vnworthy vulgar ; and which doth no
leffe commend their wifdome , than
conclude (by their contrary courfe)
our Modernes , empty , and barren of
any thing rare and pretious in them ;
who in all probability would not
proftitute all they know to the rape
and fpoile of euery illiterate reader ,
were they not confcious to themfelues their treafor deferues not many

locks to guard it vnder. But that I
may not conclude vpon a-*non concef-
fum*, for I remember I haue heard it
affirmed, (and by fome too that the
time calls Schollers), that the Auncients certainely fpoke their meanings as plaine as they could , and
were the honefter men for doing fo ;
and there may be more birds befide,of
the fame feather with thefe; therefore
I will in charity fpeake a word or two
for thefe peoples inftruction ; and in
the meane betweene the whining *He-
raclite*, and ouer rigid *Democritus* (as
much as in me lyes) *comiter erranti
monftrare viam.*

   Let fuch then as are to learne whither to conceale their knowledges ,
was the intent and ftudied purpofe
of the Auncient Poets all , and moft
of the auncient Philofophers alfo ;
let fuch I fay , know , that , when in
the worlds youth & capabler eftate ,
thofe

thofe old wife *Ægyptian* Priefts be-
ganne to fearch out the Mifteries of
Nature , (which was at firft the
whole worlds only diuinity) they de-
uized , to the end to retaine among
themfelues what they had found ,
(left it fhould be abufed and vilefied
by being deliuered to the vulgar) certaine marks,and characters of things,
vnder which all the precepts of their
wifdome were contained ; which
markes they called *Hieroglyphicks* or
facred grauings. And more then thus,
they deliuered little : or what euer it
was ,yet alwaies *disfimulanter* , and in
Enigma's and myfticall riddles , as
their following difciples alfo did.
And this prouizo of theirs , thofe I-
mages of *Sphynx* they placed before
all their Temples did infinuate ; and
which they fet for admonitions, that
high and Myfticall matters fhould
by riddles and enigmaticall knotts be
kept

kept inuiolate from the prophane
Multitude. I will giue inftance of
one or two of them. The authentike
teftimony late cited (to other purpofe)by mee of *Orpheus*,and his learning , (viz. That he was one of the
prifcæ fapientiæ patres, and that the *Secreta de numeris doctrina* and what euer
the Greeke Philofophy had in it-
Magnum & fublime , did trom his In-
ftitutions , *ut a primo fonte manare* ,)
hath thefe words immediately fol-
lowing-*Sed qui erat veterum mos philo-
fophorum* ,*ita Orpheus fuorum dogmatum
myfteria fabularum intexit inuolucris* , *&
poetico velamento disfimulauit*; *ut fi quis
legat illos Hymnos nihil fubeffe credat præ-
ter fabellas nugàfque meracisfimas*-but as
it was the manner of the Auncient
Philofophers , fo *Orpheus* within the
foults and inuoluements of fables,hid
the mifteries of his doctrine; and dif-
fembled the vnder a poeticke maske;
fo

fo as who reades thofe hymnes of his,
will not beleeue any thing to bee included vnder them, but meere tales
and trifles. *Homer* likewife, by the
fame mouth pofitiuely auerred to
haue included in his two Poems of
Iliads and *Odiſſes-all intellectuall contem-*
plation ; and which are called the Sun
and Moone of the Earth, for the light
they beare (as one well notes) before
all Learning ; (and of which *Demo-*
critus fpeaking, (as *Farra* * the *Alex-* *In Settena:*
andrian obferues) fayes-*it was impoſ-* *fol.* 259.
fible but Homer, to haue compoſed ſo won-
derfull workes, muſt haue been indued with
a diuine and inſpired nature; who vnder
a curious, and pleaſing vaile of fable, hath
taught the world how great and excellent
the beauty of true wiſdome is. no leſſe
then *Ang: Politianus* who fayes*-Om-* * *In Ambra:*
nia in his, & ab his ſunt omnia.) yet what
appeares(I fay)in thefe workes of *Ho-*
mer to the meere ; or ignorant reader,
at

at all of doctrine or document , or
more, than two fictious impossible
tales, or lyes of many men that neuer
were , and thousands of deedes that
neuer were done ? Nor lesse cautious
than these , were most of the Auncient Philosophers also. The diuine
Plato writing to a friend of his *de su-*
premis subftantijs-Per ænigmata (sayes
he) *dicendum eft : ne si epiftola fortè ad a-*
liorum peruenerit manus , quæ tibi scribi-
*mus, ab alijs intelligantur-*we must write
in enigma's and riddles, left if it come
to other hands , what wee-write to
thee,be vnderftood by others. *Ariftotle*

*In Noct:
Atnic:* of those his books,wherein he treates
of Supernaturall things , sayes (as
Aulus Gellius teftifies)* that-*they were-*
editi , & non editi; as much as to say ,
Myftically or enigmatically written;
adding farther-*cognobiles ijs tantum e-*
*runt qui nos audiunt-*they shall be only
knowne to our hearers or difciples.
                                    and

and this clofeneffe *Pythagoras* alfo hauing learned of thofe his Mafters, and
taught it his difciples, he was made
the Mafter of Silence. And who, as
all the doctrines hee deliuered were
(after the manner of the *Hebrewes,Æ-
gyptians*, and moft auncient Poets,)
layd downe in enigmaticall and figu-
ratiue notions, fo one among other of
his is this-*Giue not readily thy right hand
to euery one*, by which Precept (fayes
the profound *Iamblicus**) that great
Mafter aduertifeth that wee ought
not to communicate to vnworthy
mindes, and not yet practized in the
vnderftanding of occulte doctrines,
thofe mifterious inftructions that are
only to bee opened (fayes he) and
taught to facred and fublime wits,
and fuch as haue beene a long time
exercifed and verfed in them.

    Now, from this meanes that the
firft auncients vfed, of deliuering their

        *In lib: de
        Mifter:*

know-

knowledges thus among themselues
by word of mouth ; and by succeſſiue
reception from them downe to after
ages, That Art of myſticall writing
by Numbers, wherein they couched
vnder a fabulous attire, thoſe their
verball Inſtructions, was after, called
Scientia Cabala, or the Science of reception : *Cabala* among the *Hebrews*
ſignifying no other than the Latine
receptio : A learning by the auncients
held in high eſtimation and reuerence
and not without great reaſon ; for if
God (as the excellent *Io : Picus* * re-
hearſes)-*nibil caſu , ſed omnia per ſuam
ſapientiam vt in pondere & menſura, ita
in numero diſpoſuit* ; did nothing by
chance , but through his wiſdome
diſpoſed all things as in weight and
meaſure, ſo likewiſe in number;(and
which taught the ingenious *Saluſte* to
ſay, * that,---

*In Apolog.
fol. 115.*

*Sigr. du
Bertas* in his
Columnes.

Sacred

─────────*Sacred harmony*
And law of Number *did accompany*
Th' allmighty most, when first his ordināce
Appointed Earth to rest, and Heauen to
      daunce)

Well might *Plato* * confequently af-   * *In Epime-*
firme that-*among all liberall Arts, and*   *nide.*
contemplatiue Sciences, the chiefest and
most diuine was the-Scientia numerandi.
and who likewife queftioning why
Man was the wifeft of Animalls,
anfwers himfelfe againe (as *Ariftotle*
in his Problemes obferues)-*quia nume-*
rare nouit-becaufe hee could number.
no leffe than *Auenzoar* the *Babylonian*,
whofe frequent word by *Albumazars*
report (as *Picus Mirandula* * notes)   * *In Apo-*
was-*eum emnia noffe qui nouerat nume-*   *log:*
rare-that hee knowes all things that
knowes number. But howfoeuer an
Art thus highly cried vp by the Auncients ; Yet a Learning (I fay) now
more than halfe loft ; or at leaft by
      F 2   fuch

such as posseffe any limbe of it, rather talked of, th̃ taught. *Rabanus* a great Doctor of the Christian Church only excepted, who hath writ a particular booke-*de Numerorum virtutibus.* by diuerse others, as *Ambrose, Nazianzen, Origine, Augustine,* and many more, (as the learned *Io: Picus* at large in his Apology showes) reuerendly mentioned, but neuer published in their writings. And I am fully of opinion (which till I find reason to recant, I will not bee ashamed to owne) that the Ignorance of this Art, and the worlds mayme in the want, or not vnderstanding of it, is infinuated in the Poets generally-sung fable of *Orpheus* : whom they faigne to haue recouered his *Euridice* from Hell, with his Musick ; that is Truth and Equity, from darkenesse of Barbarisme and Ignorance, with his profound and excellent Doctrines ; but,

that

that in the thick*e* caliginous way to
the vpper-earth, fhe was loft againe;
and remaines loft to vs , that read and
vnderftand him not, for want, meerely of the knowledge of that Art of
Numbers that fhould vnlocke and
explane his Myfticall meanings to
vs.

This Learning of the *Ægyptians*
(thus concealed by them , as I haue
fhewed) being transferred from them
to the *Greekes*; was by them from
hand to hand deliuered ftill in fabulous riddles among them ; and thence
downe to the *Latines*. Of which
beades, the ingenious *Ouid* has made a
curious and excellent chaine; though
perhaps hee vnderftood not their
depth ; as our wifeft Naturalifts
doubt not to affirme, his other Con-
treymen *Lucretius*, and that more learned Scholler (I meane Imitater) of
Hefiod , the fingular *Virgil*, did ; and
which

which are the finewes and marrow ,
no leſſe than ſtarres and ornaments
of his incomparable Poems : And
ſtill by them , as by their maſters before them , preſerued with equall
care , from the miſchiefe of diuulga-
tion , or Prophanation: a vice by the
Auncients in generall , no leſſe than
by *Moſes* particularly , in the deliuering of the Law (according to the o-
pinions of the moſt learned , both
Chriſtian Diuines , and Iewiſh Ra-
bines) with ſingular caution proui-
ded againſt and auoided. *Write* (ſaid
the Angell to *Eſdras*) * *all theſe things*
that thou haſt ſeene , in a booke , and hide
them, and teach them only to the wiſe of the
people, whoſe heartes thou knoweſt may
comprehend and keep theſe ſecrets. And
ſince I late mentioned that great Se-
cretary of God , *Moſes*, to whoſe ſacred pen as we cannot attribute too
much , ſo , that wee may giue the
greater

*Lib:2. ca:
2: ver:37,*

greater reuerence to him , and confequently the greater credit to the au-
thority of thofe Auncient followers
and imitaters of his , or (that I may
righter fay , and not vnreuerently)
thofe iointrunners with him in the
fame example of clofeneffe , and care
to conceale , I will fpeake a word or
two of him. And vpon the warrant
of greater vnderftandings than my
owne , auerre , That it is the firme
opinion of all ancient writers, which
(as an indubitable troth) , they do all
with one mouth confirme , that the
full and entire knowledge of all wifdome both diuine & humane, is included in the five bookes of the *Mofaicke*
law-*disfimulata autem , & occultata* (as
the excellent *Io: Picus* in his learned* *In Heptap:
expofition vpon him fayes) *in literis
ipfis , quibus dictiones legis contexta funt-*
But hidden and difguized euen in the
letters themfelues that forme the precepts

cepts of the Law. And the same *Picus*, in * another discourse of his vpon the bookes of *Moses* more at large to the same purpose sayes-*Scribunt non modo celebres Hebræorū doctores*(whom afterwards he names , * as) *Rabi Eliazar, Rabi Moysis de Ægypto , Rabi Simeon Ben Lagis, Rabi Ismahel, Rabi Iodam, & Rabi Nachinan ; sed ex nostris quoque Esdras , Hilarius, & Origines , Mosem non legem modo , quam quinque exaratam libris posteris reliquit, sed secretiorem quoque, & veram legis enarrationem in monte diuinitus accepisse. Præceptum autem ei a Deo , vt legem quidem populo publicaret , legis autem interpretationem nec traderet literis nec inuulgaret , sed ipse Iesu Naue tantum ; tum ille , alijs deinceps sacerdotum primoribus, magna silentij religione reuelaret*-the most renowned and authétique not only among the Hebrew Doctors , as *Rabi Eliazar , Rabi Moysis de Ægypto , Rabi Symeon &c.* but among

* In Apolog: fo: 81.

* Fo: 116.

among ours alfo , *Efdras, Hillary* , and *Origine* , doe write that *Mofes* recei-ued from God vpon the mount not the Law only , which he hath left in fiue bookes exactly deliuered to po-fterity , but the more hidden alfo, and true explanation of the Law : But with all , was warned and commaun-ded by God , that as he fhould pu-blifh the Law to the People , fo the interpretation thereof , he fhould nei-ther commit to letters nor diuulge ; but he to *Iofua* only and *Iofua* to the o-ther fucceeding primaries among the Priefts ; and that , vnder a great religi-on of fecrecy. and concludes-*Et meri-to quidem; Nam fatis erat vulgaribus , & per fimplicem hiftoriam nunc Dei potenti-am, nunc in improbos iram , in bonos cle-mentiam , in omnes iuftitiam agnofcere, & per diuina falutariàque præcepta , ad bene beatèque viuendum & cultum relligionis inftitui ; at mifteria fecretiora , & fub cor-*

G

tice

tice legis rudique verborum prætextu la-
titantia altisfima diuinitatis arcana plebi
palam facere, quid erat aliud quàm dare
sanctum canibus, & inter porcos spargere
margaritas; and not without great reason; for it was enough for the multitude to be by meerely the simple story, taught and made to know, now
the Power of God, now his Wrath
against the wicked, Clemency to-
wards the good, and Iustice to all;and
by diuine and wholesome precepts in-
structed in the wayes of religion, and
holy life. But those secreter Mysteries,
and abstrusities of most high diuinity, hidden and concealed vnder the
barke, and rude couer of the words,
to haue diuulged and layd these open
to the vulgar; what had it been other
than to giue holy things to dogs, and
cast pearles among swine? So he.
And this little that I haue heere rehearsed (for in a thing so knowne to

all

all that are knowers , mee thinkes I
haue faid rather too much than otherwife) fhall ferue for inftance of *Mofes*
his myfticall manner of writing.
Which I haue the rather done for inftruction of fome ignorant , though
ftiffe oppofers of this truth , that I
haue lately met with ; but chiefely in
iuftification of thofe other wife Auncients, of his , and fucceeding times,
Poets,and Philofophers,that were no
leffe carefull then *Mofes* was , not to
giue-*Sanctum canibus* , (as before faid)
nor *inter porcos fpargere margaritas.*

Now to go about to examine whither it appeares our Modernes (Poets
efpecially , for I will exempt diuerfe
late profe-writers), haue any the like
clofeneffe as before mentioned ; were
a worke fure as vaine and vnneceffary,
as it is a truth firme and vnqueftio-
nable, that they poffeffe the knowledge of no fuch myfteries as deferue

G 2   the

the vfe of any art at all for their concealing.

3. The laft, and greateft difparity,
and wherein aboue all others, the
groffeft defect and maime appeares,
in our Modernes (and efpecially Poets) in refpect of the Auncients; is
their generall ignoráce, euen throughout all of them, in any the myfteries and hidden properties of Nature;
which as an vnconcerning Inquifition
it appeares not in their writings they
haue at all troubled their heads with.
Poets I faid efpecially (and indeed only) for we haue many Profe-men excellent naturall Philofophers in thefe
late times; and that obferue ftrictly
that clofeneffe of their wife Mafters
the reuerend Auncients; So as now
a dayes our Philofophers are all our
Poets, or what our Poets fhould bee;
and our Poefies growne to bee little
better than fardles of fuch fmall ware

as

as thofe Marchants the French call
pedlers, carry vp and downe to fell;
whisfles, painted rattles, and fuch
like *Bartholmew*-babyes. for what o-
ther are our common vninftructing
fabulous rimes, then amufements for
fooles and children? But our Rimes
(fay they) are full of Morall doctrine.
be it fo. But why not deliuered then
in plaine profe, and as openly to euery
mans vnderftanding, as it deferues to
be taught, and commonly knowne
by euery one. The Auncients (fay
they) were Authors of Fables, which
they fung in meafured numbers, as
we in imitation of them do. True:
but fure enough their meanings were
of more high nature, and more difficult to be found out, then any booke
of Manners wee fhall readily meete
withall, affoordes; elfe they had not
writ them fo obfcurely, or we fhould
find them out more eafily, and make
                              fome

fome vfe of them : whereas not vnderftanding nor feeking to vnderftand
them, we make none at all. Wee liue
in a myfte, blind and benighted ; and
fince our firft fathers difobedience
poyfoned himfelfe and his pofterity,
Man is become the imperfecteft and
moft deficient Animall of all the
field : for then he loft that Inftinct
that the Beaft retaines ; though with
him the beaft, and with it the whole
vegitable and generall Terrene nature
alfo fuffered , and ftill groanes vnder
the loffe of their firft purity, occafio-
ned by his fall. What concernes him
now fo neerely as to attend to the cul-
tiuating or refining,& thereby aduan-
cing of his rationall part , to the purchafe & regaining of his firft loft feli-
city? And what meanes to conduce to
this purchafe, can there bee , but the
knowledge firft , and loue next (for
none can loue but what hee firft
knowes)

knowes)of his Maker,for whofe loue
and feruice he was only made? And
how can this blind, lame, and vtterly
imperfeƈt Man, with fo great a lode
to boote of originall and aƈtuall of-
fence vpon his back, hope to approach this fupreme altitude, and im-
menfity, which

———*In quella inacceßibil luce,*

Quaſi in alta caligine s'aſconde,

(as an excellent Poeteſſe * difcribes
the infcrutable Beeing of God) but
by two meanes only : the one, by lay-
ing his burden on him that on his
Croſſe bore the burthen of all our de-
feƈtes,and interpofitions betweene vs
and the hope of the vifion of his blef-
fed Eſſence face to face heereafter;
and the other, by carefull fearche of
him here in this life (according to
Saint *Paules* inftruƈtion),in his works;
who telles vs *-thofe inuifible things of
God are cleerely feene, being vnderftood*
by

* *La Sig.ra
vitto: Colona na.*

* *Rom:cap:1.
ver: 20.*

by the things that are made; or by the workes of his bleſſed hands? So as, betweene theſe two mayne and only meanes of acquiring here the knowledge, and hereafter the viſion of him wherein all our preſent and future happineſſe conſiſts, what middle place (to deſcend to my former diſcourſe) can theſe mens Morall Philoſophy (trow we) challenge? which in its firſt Maſters and teachers time, before there was any better diuinity knowne, might well enough paſſe for a courſe kind of diuinity; but howeuer, ſuch a one, as (with the leaue of our Poets) needes no fiction to clothe or conceale it in. And therfore vtterly vnfit to bee the Subiect of Poems: ſince it containes in it but the obuious reſtraints or impulſions of the Humane Sence and will, to or from what it ynly before-hand (without extrinſicke force or law) feeles

and

and knowes it ought to fhunne, or imbrace. The other two more remooued and harder leſſons do certainely
more in the affaire both of ſoule and
body, concerne vs. And theſe (if we
be wiſe enough to loue our ſelues ſo
well), wee muſt ſeeke and take from
the hands of their fitteſt teachers.
As, in the firſt, we need goe no farther (though learned & wiſe Writers
haue made mention, and to high purpoſe, of a *Theologia Philoſophica*, as they
call ſome of the doctrines of the auncient Poets) then to the Doctors, and
Doctrines of that Church that God
dyed to plant, and which ſhall liue
till the worlds death. And for inſtruction in our next neceſſary Leſ-
ſon, to wit, the Miſteries of Nature,
we muſt, if we will follow *Plato's*
aduice-*inquire of thoſe* (and by them
be directed) *who liued neereſt to the time
of the gods*; meaning the old wiſe

H   Ethnicks:

Ethnicks : among whom , the best
Masters were certainly most, if not
all of them , Poets ; and from whose
fires (as I haue formerly touched) the
greatest part of all humane knowledges haue taken their first light. A-
mong these , I say , and not elsewhere
(excepting the sacred Old Law only) must we search for the knowledge of the wise , and hidden wayes
& workings of our great Gods hand-
maid, Nature. But alas who findes ,
or who seekes now adayes to finde
them? Nay (what is more strange)
there want not of these learned of our
times , that will not bee intreated
to admit those excellent Masters of
knowledge to meane (if they allow
them any meaning) scarce other at
all,then meerely Morall doctrine.

I haue knowne Latine and Greeke
Interpreters of them in these times;
men otherwise of much art,and such

as

as able to render their Authors phrafe
to the height of their good , in our
worfe language ; yet aske the moft ,
as I haue fome of them , and I feare
they will anfwere, as one (and the
beft) of our Greeke tranflators hath
ingenuoufly confeft to mee , that for
more then matter of Morality , hee
hath difcouered little in his Authors
meanings. Yet my old good friend as
well as I wifh him, (and very well I
wifh him for thofe parts of Fancy,In-
duftry, and meritorious Ability that
are in him) muft pardon mee that I
affirme, it is not truer that there euer
was fuch a thing as a *Mufæus* , or *He-*
fiod , or *Homer* , whom he has taught
to fpeake excellent Englifh ; then
it is, that the leaft part of the Doctrine (or their wifeft expofitors a-
bufe mee, and other Ignorants with
mee) that they meant to lay downe
in thofe their wife,though impoffible

fables

fables, was matter of Manners, but chiefely Nature: No leſſe then in the reſt of thoſe few before, and many after them, whom all Antiquity has cried vp for excellent Poets, and called their works perfect Poems.

For proofe of which Truth; wee will firſt mention two or three of the beſt of them; and to omit the multiplicity of leſſe autentike teſtimonies, that all Authors are full of, alledge only the beforecited *Mirandula*, who ſpeaking of that *Magia naturalis*, or naturall wiſdome, or as he defines it *exacta & abſoluta cognitio omnium rerum naturàlium*-the exact and abſolute knowledge of all naturall things (which the Auncients were Maſters of) ſayes, * that in that Art (among ſome others he mentions) *Praſtitit Homerus*, Homer excelled; and who-*vt omnes alias ſapientias, ita hanc quoq; ſub ſui Vlyxis erroribus diſſimulauit*-as all other know-

* *In Apolog: fo: 112.*

* *Ibid: fo: 80.*

knowledge, so hath hiddenly layd downe this also in his *Ulysses* his trauailes. As likewise of *Orpheus*-*Nihil efficacius Hymnis Orphei in naturali Magia, si debita musica, animi intentio, & cœteræ circumstantiæ quas nôrunt sapientes fuerint adhibitæ* : There is nothing of greater efficacy then the hymnes of *Orpheus* in naturall Magick, if the fitting musick, intention of the minde, and other circumstances which are knowne to the wise, bee considered and applyed. And againe*-*that they are of no lesse power in naturall magick*, or to the vnderstanding thereof, *then the Psalmes of Dauid are in the Caball*, or to vnderstand the *Cabalistick* Science by. And lastly, *Zoroaster*; who that he was a possessor likewise of that-*absoluta cognitio rerum Naturalium* before mētioned, no lesse then of that *Theologicall Philosophy* his expounders find in him, may appeare by that Doctrine

of

* *In Conclus.*

* *Ibid:*

of his (in particular) of the-*Scala à Tartaro ad primum ignem*, which the learned *Io: Picus* interprets*-*Seriem naturarum vniuerfi à non gradu materia, ad eum qui eft fuper omnem gradum graduatè protenfum*-the feries or concatenation of the vniuerfall Natures, from a no degree (as he fpeakes) of matter, to him that is aboue or beyond all degree graduately extended; no leffe then by that Attribute (in generall) giuen him by all the learned of all Ages; *viz*: that he was one of the greateft (as firft) of Naturall Magicians, or Mafters of the abfolute knowledge of all Nature.

To omit (as I faid) the Teftimonies of an infinity of other Authors in confirmation of the before-affirmed troth; who knowes not, that moft, if not all of thofe fables in all the reft of the Auncients, of their gods and goddeffes efpecially, with the

* *In Conclu:*

the affinities, entercourſes, and com-
merces betweene themſelues, and
with others; (of which, as *Homer*,
that Greeke Oracle is abūdantly full,
ſo the reſt, as a *Heſiod*, *Linus* the
Maſter, and *Muſæus* the Scoller of *Or-*
pheus, and (as we haue ſaid) *Zoroaſter*,
and *Orpheus* himſelfe, and all thoſe
moſt aunciént, (if we may beleeue
their beſt expounders and relaters of
moſt we haue of them) made the
maine grounds and Subiects of their
writings;) who knowes not (I ſay)
that moſt, if not all, of thoſe their
fables of this kinde, and which haue
of all learned, in all ages, been chiefely tearmed Poetick, & fitteſt matter
for Poeſy; haue neuer been by any
wiſe expounder made to meane other
then meerely the Generation of the
Elements, with their Vertues, and
Changes; the Courſes of the Starres,
with their Powers, and Influences;
and

and all the moſt important Secrets
of Nature, hanging neceſſarily vpon
the knowledge of Theſe ; which
could not ſuffer ſo ſimple a Relation
as the Ethick doctrine requires ; becauſe by the vulgarity of Thoſe,
much miſchiefe muſt in all reaſon
enſue ; being (alſo) of thoſe tenderer
things, that are ſooneſt prophaned &
vilefied by their cheapneſſe ; & This,
cannot for the generall benefit of
mankinde be among the plaineſt of
leſſons too commonly knowne and
openly diuulged to euery body.

I will not deny but the Auncients
mingled much doctrine of Morality
(yea, high Diuinity alſo) with their
Naturall Philoſophy ; as the late
mentioned *Zoroaſter* firſt ; who hath
diuinely ſung of the Eſſence and at-
tributes of God. and was (as the learned *Farra* auouches) *-*the firſt Au-*
thor of that Religious Philoſophy , or Phi-
loſophicall

* In Settena:
fo: 57.

losophicall Religion, that was after followed & amplified by Mercurius Trismegistus, Orpheus, Aglaophemus, Pythagoras, Eudoxus, Socrates, Plato, &c. And Orpheus next; who, as he writt particular bookes; of Astrology, first (as Lucian* tells vs) of any man; as also of diseases and their cures; of the natures and qualities of the Elements; of the force of Loue or agreemét in Naturall things; and many more that we read of, besides his Hymnes which are perhaps the greatest part of what now remaines of him heere among vs: so his expounders likewise find in him that Theologia Philosophica as they call it, which they giue to Zoroaster. Witnesse Pausanias, who reports * -Orpheus multa humanæ politicæque vitæ vtilia inuenit: & vniuersam Theologiam primus aperuit, & nefariorum facirorum expiationes excogitauit, &c. But let vs heare how himselfe *sings; and which

*In Dialog: de Astrol:

*In Bœotic:

* In Lib: de verbo sacro.

I   is

is by *Eusebius Pamphilus*, in his honour rehearsed *.

*Lib: 13.de
Præp:Euan-
gel:

*O you that vertue follow, to my sense
Bend your attentiue minds : Prophane
   ones hence.
And thou Musæus, who alone the shine
Highly contemplat'st of the formes di-
   uine,
Learne my notes; which with th'inward
    eye behold,*   *(hold.
And vntouch'd in thy sacred bosome
Incline thee by my safe-aduizing verse
To the high Author of this Vniuerse.
One only, all immortall, (such is he;
Whose Being I discouer thus to thee;
This alone-perfect, this eternall King
Rais'd aboue all, created eu'ry thing,
And all things gouernes. with the Spirit
   alone
(Not otherwise) to be beheld, or knowne.
From him no ill springs. there's no god
   but he.*   *(dently;
Thinke now, and looke about thee pru-*

                      And

And better to difcouer him , loe I
His tracts and footfteps vpon earth ,⎫
   and high   (crie;⎬
Strong hand behold,but cǎnot him def-⎭
Who (to an vnimaginable height
Rais'd) in darke clouds conceales him
   from my fight.
Only a Caldean *faw him;and the grace
Hath now aloft to view him face to face.
His facred right hand grafpes the Oce-
   an ; and
Touch'd with it , the proud mountaines
   trembling ftand
Eu'n from the deep rootes to their vt-
   moft height :
Nor feeles at all th'immenfneße of their
   weight,
He, who aboue the heau'n doth dwell,yet
   guides
And gouernes all that vnder heau'n a-
   bides.   (extend;
O're all, through all doth his vaft power
Of th'Vniuerfe beginning,midds, & end.

*Meaning fure *Mofes*; who the holy writ faies. *Saw God face to face.* vnleffe with *Eufebius*, we will haue him meane the*Patriarke* *Abraham*.

And as thefe two diuine Authors in particular, fo likewife among the reft of the Auncient Poets in generall , I will graunt they haue in their Poefies (as I haue faid) mingled much Morality with their Ethick doctrines. As in their *Hercules, Thefeus, Vlyffes, Æneas,* and other their Heröes they haue giuen example of all vertues ; and punifht all vices ; as pride and ambition , in their *Giants* and *Titanes, &c.* Contempt of the gods, in their *Niobe, Arachne, Caffiope, Medufa, Amphion, Marfyas,* the *Mineides, &c.* murder, luft, couetife, and the reft, in their *Lycaon, Ixion, Sifyphus, Midas, Tantalus, Titius, &c.* Yet queftionleffe infinite many more of their fables then thefe, (though euen thefe and the reft of this kind want not among our beft Mythologians their Phyfick, as well as Ethick meanings,) as all thofe of their gods and goddeffes ,

with

with their powers and dignies, and all paſſage of affinity and commerce betweene themſelues, and betweene them and others, were (as I haue ſaid before) made to meane meere matter of Nature ; and in no poſſibility of Senſe to bee wreſted to the doctrine of Manners,vnleſſe a man will(with-all) bee ſo inhumane as to allow all thoſe riotts,rapes,murders,adulteries, inceſtes, and thoſe *nefaria* and *nefanda*, vnnaturally-ſeeming vices that they tell of them, to bee (litterally or Morally taken) fit examples of Man-ners, or wholeſome inſtructions for the liues of men to be leuelled and di-rected by.

Whereas , on the contrary ſide , (that I may inſtance ſome of them) who can make that Rape of *Proſer-pine*, whom her mother *Ceres* (that vnder the Species of Corne might in-clude as well the whole Genus of the
                                        Vege-

Vegetable nature) fought fo long for
in the earth, to meane other, then the
putrefaction, and fucceeding generation of the Seedes we commit to *Pluto*, or the earth ? whome they make
the God of wealth, calling him alfo
Dis quafi diues (the fame in Latine
that *Pluto* is in Greeke) rich, or weal-
thy, becaufe all things haue their originall from the earth, and returne to
the earth againe. Or what can *Iupiters*
blafting of his beloued *Semele*, after
his hauing defloured her, and the
wrapping of his fonne he got on her
(*Bacchus*, or wine) in his thigh after
his production, meane other then the
neceffity of the Ayres heate to his
birth, in the generation ; and (after a
violent preffure and dilaceration of
his mother the Grape) the like clofe
imprifoning of him alfo, in a fit vef-
fell, till he gaine his full maturity,
and come to be fit aliment ?

After

After thefe two particular fcanda-
lous fables, and which I will call but
inferiour fpeculations, yet neceffary
documents, becaufe, of the Natures
of Corne, and Wine, the *Suftentacula
vitæ*; (To omit the Adultery of *Mars*
and *Venus*, by which the Chymifts
will haue meant the infeperability of
thofe two Metals that carry their
names; witneffe that exuberance of
Venus-or copper which wee call *Vi-
triole*, that is feldome or neuer found
without fome mixture more or leffe
of *Mars* or iron in it; as her husband
Vulcan, or materiall fire findes and
fhewes the practitioners in Chymi-
ftry. And with this, other alfo of the
like obuioufer kinde of truths in Nature; as *Hebe's* ftumbling and falling
with the Nectar-bowle in her hand,
and thereby difcouering her hidden
parts to the gods, as fhe ferued them
at their boord; meaning the naked-
nefle

neſſe of the trees and plants in Au-
tumne, when all their leaues are falne
from them by the downefall or de-
parture of the *Spring* , which their
Hebe , or *goddeße* of *youth* as the
Auncients called her (becauſe the
Spring renewes and makes young all
things) meanes. And with theſe, the
Inceſte of Mirrha with her father;
meaning the Myrrh-tree, which the
Sun (father of Plants) inflames,
and making ouertures in it , there
flowes thence that odorous *Sabæan*
gumme wee call Myrrhe, (meant by
her child *Adonis*, which interpreted is
ſweet, pleaſant, or delightfull.) To
omit (I ſay) theſe, and the like triui-
aller (though true) obſeruations in
Nature ; and that carry alſo ſo foule a
face to the eye; I would aske who
can make thoſe fights and contenti-
ons that the wiſe *Homer* faignes betweene his Gods and Goddeſſes to
meane

meane other then the naturall Con-
trariety of the Elements : and especially of the Fire and Water ; which
as they are tempered and reconciled
by the aire, so *Iuno* (which signifies
the aery region) reconciles,& accords
the warring Gods. and next, what in
generall those frequent, and no lesse
scandalous brawles betweene *Iupiter*
and (his wife and sister) *Iuno*, can be
made to meane other, then those
Meteors occasioned by the vpper and
lower Région of the Ayres differing
temperatures ; Or what all those his
vnlawfull loues, his compressing so
many *Dryads*, *Nayads*, and *Nereiads*
(woodnymphes,and waternymphes)
and the rest, can meane other then
meerely the Fires power vpon the
Earth, and waters ; (a study of
a higher nature and vaster extente
then the first alledged) and which
Iupiters Inceste with his sister *Ceres*

likewife meanes;and is the fame with
the tale of the contention of *Phaëton*
which is *Incendium*, with the fonne
of *Ifis* which is *Terra*.

A Theame too infinite to purfue;
and no leffe a fault heere, then (perhaps) a folly at all to mencion : For
(befides the beeing a fubiect vtterly
vnfit to fuffer a mixture with a difcourfe of fo light a nature as this
of mine , where a flight touch
at the generall miftake and abufe of
Poefy in our times,was only intended)
fuppofe a man fhould (wheras I haue
heere layd downe the faire fenfe of
but two or three of the foulest of
them) be at the paines of running
through all the Fables of the Auncients, and out of them fhew the
reader , and leade him by the fingar
as it were (who yet can difcouer nothing but matter of Manners in them)
to the fpeculation of the entire Secret
of

of our great God of Nature , in his
miraculous fabrick of this World ,
(which , their god *Pan* , or the
vniuerfall fimple bodyes, and feedes
of all Nature , gotten by *Mercu-*
ry or the diuine Will, by which all
things came to bee created, meanes;)
And (beginning with *Mofes*)
fhew him how the Spirit of God
firft moouing vpon the waters (a
Myftery perhaps by few of our dul-
ler Modernes vnderftood, though a
Thales Milefius,or *Heraclius* the Ephe-
fian , two Heathens, could inftruct
them) they faigne him vnder the
name of *Iupiter* , by compreffing *La-*
tona (meaning the fhades or darke-
neffe of the firft *Chäos*) to haue begot
on her, *Apollo* and *Diana*,which is the
Sun and Moone, when he faid *fiat lux*,
& lux fuit , and carry him along from
this beginning to the end and compleate knowledge of all Nature ,

(which

which as *Mofes* darkely, they no
leffe darkely deliuered;) Suppofe (I
fay) a man fhould take this taske
vpon him, I would faine know who
they are that would be perhaps, at
leaft, that were, fit readers now a
dayes of fuch a Treatife? Becaufe
what one of a million of our Scollers
or writers among vs, vnderftands, or
cares to be made vnderftand fcarfe
the loweft and triuialleft of Natures
wayes?much leffe feekes to draw (by
wifely obferuing her higher and more
hidden workings) any profitabler vfe
or benefit from them, for their owne,
or the publike good, then perhaps
to make an Almanack, or a diuing-
bote to take butts or crabs vnder water with; or elfe fome Douch water-
bellowes, by rarefying water into a
compreft ayre to blow the fire with-
all?

Whenas if they could, but from
that

that poore ftep , learne the way to get a little higher vp the right fcale of Nature, and really indeed accord , and make a firme peace and agreement betweene all the difcordant Elements; and (as the Fable of *Cupids* wrafsle with *Pan*, and ouercomming him , teaches them the beginning of all Natures productions are loue and ftrife,) indeauour to irritate alfo , and force this *Pan*, or Simple Matter of things to his fit procreatiue ability , by an induftrious and wife ftrife and colluctation with him ; then they might perhaps do fomewhat in Philofophy not vnworth the talking of. No leffe then our common practitioners in Phyfick might better deferue their names then moft of them do ; (for to be a Phyfitian , what is it but to be a generall Naturalift,not meere tranfcriber and applyer of particular booke-*recipes* ?) if they would
but

but practife, by that Rule and Bafe of
Nature the world was built vpon, to
make likewife and eftablifh that E-
quality and concord betweene thofe
warring Elements (which are the
Complexions) in Mans body, that
one exceed not an other in their Qualities: Or if they could but giue better
inftance of their acquaintance with
the wayes of Phylofophy, then in
burdning and oppreffing nature, rather then otherwife, as moft of them
doe, with their crude Vegetable and
Minerall Phyficks, for not vnderftanding the neceffity, (or though
they did, yet not the Art) of exalting
and bettering their natures, by corre-
cting or remoouing their in-bred
imperfections, with that fit prepa-
ration that Nature teaches them.

The hidden workings of which
wife Miftreffe, could wee fully in all
her wayes comprehend, how much
would

would it cleare, and how infinitely
ennoble our blind and groueling con-
ditions, by exalting our vnderſtan-
dings to the ſight (as I haue before
toucht) of God, or-*thoſe inuiſible things
of God* (to vſe S. *Pauls* words once a-
gaine) *which are cleerely ſeene, being vn-
derſtood by the things that are made*; and
thence inſtructing vs, not ſawcily to
leap, but by the linkes of that golden
chaine of *Homer*, that reaches from
the foote of *Iupiters* throne to the
Earthe, more knowingly, and conſe-
ſequently more humbly climbe vp
to him, who ought to bee indeed
the only end and period of all our
knowledge, and vnderſtanding. the
which in vs though but a ſmall
fainte beame of that our great bleſſed *Sun*, yet is that breath of life
that he breathed into vs, to draw vs
thereby (*feciſti nos Domine propter te*;
ſayes the holy S. *Auguſtine*) * neerer   * *In Confeſſ:*
                                          to

to him, then all irrationall Animalls of his making; as a no lesse tenderly louing Father, then immense and omnipotent Creator.

To whom as wee cannot giue too much loue and reuerence; so neither can wee with too wary hands approach his sacred Mysteries in Holy Writ. Howbeit I must (to returne home to my former discourse) in honour & iust praise of the before mentioned wise Auncients (and with the premised befitting caution) not doubt to say, that as his Instructions in the holy Scripture, and especially in the old Law, must of necessity reach as far farther then the bare historicall trueth (though not in the same manner) as extends the difference in our selues betweene Nature alone, and Nature and Grace vnited; so likewise, that one, and a great portion of the doctrine of that part of holy Writ, the

the wife Ethnicks vndoubtedly pof-
feſt in all perfection ; to wit , the
knowledge of all Natures moſt high
and hidden wayes and workings : and
though far ſhort in the ſafer part of
wiſdome , of their more inlightned
ſucceſſors , yet was the bare light (or
rather fire) of nature in them, enough
to draw thē as high as Reaſon could
help fleſh and bloud to reach heauen
with. Nay which is more, were it not
wide of my purpoſe (though it con-
tradicts it not) to conſter them other
then meere children of Nature , I
might perhaps gaine fauour of ſome
of our weaker perſuaders in their ſpi-
rituall Cures (if to flanke and ſtreng-
then the diuine letter with prophaner
Authorities, be in this backward and
incredulous age , not irrequiſite) by
paralelling in the Hiſtoricall part I
meane chiefely, and as it lies, the Sacred letter and Ethnick Poeſyes to-
L gether

gether to a large extention : And beginning with *Moses*, shew them, all
those-*dij maiorum gentium* from *Saturne*
to *Deucalions* deluge, were but names
for *Adam*, *Caine*, *Lamech* and the
rest of their successors to *Noahs* floud:
Nor that their *Rhæa* (or *Terra*, mother of all the Gods) and *Venus*,
could be other then *Moses* his *Eua* and
Lib:1.Oper: & dier: Noema. What other can *Hesiod's* * *Pan-dora-the first and beautifullest of all wo-men,by whome all euils were dispersed and spred vpon the Earth*, meane then *Moses*
his *Eue* ? What can *Homers* *Ate*,
Ilia: lib:19. whom he calls* the first daughter of
Iupiter, and a woman pernicious and
harmefull to all vs mortalls;and in an
other place tells how the wisest of
men was cosened and deceiued by his
wife ; what can he I say, meane in
these women but *Eue*? What was the
Poets *Bacchus* but his *Noah*, or *Noa-chus*, first corrupted to *Boachus*,and after,

ter, by remoouing a letter, to *Bacchus*;
who, (as *Mofes* tels vs of *Noah*,) was the
firft likewife in their accompt, that
planted the vine, and taught men the
vfe of wines foone after the vniuerfall
deluge ? What can be plainer then
that by their *Ianus* they ment *Noah* alfo, whome they giue two faces to,
for hauing feene both the old and
new world; and which, his name (in
Hebrew, *Iain*, or wine) likewife con-
firmes; *Noah* being (as we late alledged *Mofes* for witneffe) the firft in-
uentor of the vfe of wines ? What
could they meane by their *Golden-
Age*, when--*Nulli fubigebant arua coloni*;
————*Ipfaque tellus*

Omnia liberius, nullo pofcente ferebat;
But the ftate of Man before his Sin ?
and confequently by their Iron age,
but the worlds infelicity, and miferies
that fucceeded his fall ? when————

Luctus,& vltrices posuere cubilia curæ;
Pallentesque habitant morbi, tristisque
senectus,
Et metus, & malesuada fames, & tur-
pis egestas.

Lastly, (for I haue too much already exceeded my commission) what
can *Adonis horti* among the Poets
meane other then *Moses* his *Eden*, or
terrestriall Paradise? the Hebrew *E-*
den being *Voluptas* of *Delitiæ*, whence
the Greeke ἰδονὴ (or pleasure) seemes
necessarily deriued: The *Caldæans* and
Persians (so I am tould) called it *Par-*
deis, the Greeks, παράδεισος, the *Latines*
altered the Greeke name to *Paradisus;*
which as *Eden*, is (as, * *Aulus Gellius*
defines it) *Locus amænißimus, & volup-*
tatis plenißimus; the which selfe thing
the auncient both Poets and Philosophers certainely ment by their *horti*
Hesperidum likewise.

Now though we reuerence *Moses*
more

* *In Noc:*
Attic:

more (as we ought to doe) then thefe his condifciples, becaufe infpired fo far aboue them with the immediate fpirit of Almighty God ; yet ought we neuerthelefle to reuerence them , and the wifdome of their fables, how-euer not vnderftood by euery body: his condifciples I call them , becaufe they read bothe vnder their *Ægyptian* teachers one leffon, & were (as *Mofes* of himfelfe fayes) expert in the learning of the *Ægyptians* : yea many of them (and Poets all) were (to fpeake fitly-er) the teachers of that Learning themfelues , and Mafters therein no lefle then *Mofes*. How can We then indeed attribute too much to their knowledges , though deliuered out of wife confideration in riddles and fictious tales ?

But alas (with fhame enough may we fpeake it) fo far are we now a-dayes from giuing the due to them
they

they deſerue, as thoſe their learned
and excellent fables ſeeme rather read
to be abuſed, then ſtudyed in theſe
times; and euen by people too that
are,or would be accompted profound
men.

What child of learning or louer
of Truth could abide to ſee great pretenders to learning among vs, that
doubt, and obſtinately too, whether
the pretious treaſure of that wiſdome
of the Auncients, ſo carefully by
them left ſealed vp to the vſe of their
true Heires (the wiſe and worthy of
their poſterity) be any more indeed
then a legacy of meere old wiues
tales to poyſon the world with. If
we will call this but ignorance, let vs
go farther; and ſuppoſe that a man
(nor vnlearned one neither)ſhall haue
taken paines in foure or fiue fables of
the Auncients to vnfould and deliuer
vs much doctrine and high meanings
in

in them, which he calls their wifdome ; and yet the fame man in an o-
ther Treatife of his, fhall fay of thofe
auncient Fables.-*I thinke they were firft
made, and their expofitions deuifed after-
ward*: and a little after-*Of Homer himfelfe, notwithftanding be was made a kind
of Scripture by the latter Scooles of the
Græcians, yet I fhould without any difficulty pronounce his fables had in his owne
meaning no fuch inwardneffe, &c.* What
fhall we make of fuch willing con-
tradiĉtiós, when a man to vent a few
fancies of his owne, fhall tell vs firft,
they are the wifdome of the Auncients; and next, that thofe Auncient
fables were but meere fables , and
without wifdom or meaning,til their
expofitcurs gaue them a meaning; &
then, fcornefully and contemptuouf-
ly (as if all Poetry were but Play-va-
nity) fhut vp that difcourfe of his of
Poetry, with-*It is not good to ftay too
long*

long in the Theater.

But let me not ftick too long
neither in this myre; nor feeme o-
uer-fenfible of wrong to what can
fuffer none; for-*Veritas* (fayes the holy writ) *magna eft* , *& prænalebit :* and
fuch are (nor leffe great and preuai-
ling then truth it felfe) thofe before
mentioned *Arcana* of our wife Auncients; which no Barbarifme I know
can efface ; nor all the dampes and
thick fogs by dull & durty Ignorance
breathed on them , darken at all, or
hide from the quick eye of feleƈt and
happier vnderftandings; who know
full well, the ripeft friutes of knowledge grow euer higheft; while the
lower-hanging boughs (for euery
ones gripe) are either barren, or their
fruite too fowre to be worth the gathering. And among fuch may they
euer reft , fafe wrapt vp in their
huskes , and inuoluements : And let
our

our writers write (if it can bee no
better) and Rimers rime ſtill after
their accuſtomed and moſt accepted
manner, and ſtill captiuate and rauiſh
their like hearers. Though in my
owne inclination, I could with much
iuſter alacrety, then in perſon of the
Roman Poet, with his-*Vilia miretur
vulgus*; or *Roman* Orator, with his-
Similes habent ſua labra laĉtucas (while
he laught to ſee a greedy Aſſe at his
ſutable thiſsles,)wiſh we might each
one, according to the meaſure of his
illumination, and by the direĉtion of
Gods two great bookes, that of his
law firſt, and that of the Creature
next, (wherein, to vſe the excellent
Io: Picus his phraſe*-*leguntur magnalia*
Dei-the wonderfull things of God
are read) run on together in a ſafe and
firme rode of Trueth: to the end that
vindicating ſome part of our loſt Heritage and Beatitude heere, we may
thence(an aduantage the holy *Maxi-*

*In Concluſ: *

M   *mus*

mus Tyrius * fayes the more happy
fpirits haue ouer others) arriue the
lefle Aliens and ftrangers in the Land
of our eternall Heritage, and Beatitude heereafter.

APPENDIX.

The before-written Treatife of
the dignity of the ould Poets and
their Poefies, falling into the view of
fome not iniudicious eyes; Among
them, there arofe queftion, how it
could be, that *Plato*, fo great a louer
and honorer of the Auncient Poets
in generall, and of *Homer* (one of the
beft of them) in particular; fhould
exclude and banifh him neuerthelefle
out of his *Common-wealth* : To which
is eafily and briefely anfwered, that,
as there is no Citty, corporation, or
common-wealth in the world, but
differs from all others, if not in all, at
leaft in fome particular lawes, infti-
tutions,

tutions, or cuftomes; fo, moft reafo-
nable is it , that fuch a Common-
wealth as *Plato* formes , fhould more
then any other , be differing from all
others , in new Lawes, rules , and in-
ftitutions : His intention being to
frame an affembly of men, or republike , which confifting onely of
Reafon, was rather the *Idea* of what
a perfect common-wealth fhould be,
then as eyther being , or eafy or pof-
fible to bee put into Act. Hee
formes all his Cittizens, diuine , he-
roique , and perfectly Philofophick
and wife fpirits , and fuch as are already arriued to the fumme of all intellectuall height , and perfection of
vertue and Sapience ; And therefore
can haue no need of a *Homer* or his inftructions , to fhew them the way
to bee , or make them what they are
already made : In all other Common-
wealthes, the cafe is differing ; where

Homers, *Hefiods*, *Orpheuſſes*, and thoſe Fathers of knowledge and learning, are euer neceſſary, to ailure with the ſweetneſſe and pleaſure of their fictions, the mindes of men to the loue and knowledge of vertue and wiſdome: So as, out of this reſpect meerly, and not that he was at all the leſſe worthy of honour and admiration, (in his fit place of vſe) was *Homer* exempt, and ſhut out from *Plato's* imaginary aſſembly, and excellent republike. And therefore I will conclude with *Maximus Tyrius*, who ſayes (as *Farra Alexandrinus* obſerues *)-*We ought to giue honour to Plato ; but yet ſo, as we rob not the great Homer, nor ſcante him of his due and deſerued prayſes.*

In Settemer :

F I N I S.

THE TALE OF

NARCISSVS

briefly Mythologifed,

Aduertisment to the Reader.

AFter I had writ the precedent Discourse of the value of true Poesy, and therein giuen a short generall Notion only, of the being (as I conceiued) somewhat in the fables of the Auncients, considerable, and to be esteemed aboue the multitude of the vninstructing workes of most of our Moderne Poets; I remembred my selfe of the Fable of their Narcissus, which I had diuerse yeares since, put into Euglish: and finding it not voide of his meaning, no lesse then those other the like documents deliuered in Fables by the wise Auncients for the worlds instruction; I was not vnwilliug to annexe it (together with a short obseruation vpon it) to the former Treatise: to the end the worthy louer of Trueth, finding in but this one among a million of their fables, somewhat he perhaps before, heeded (or vnderstood) not, (though a tale frequently read by euery body) he might the lesse erre in his search of humane knowledge; being prompted where it is in an ample manner to bee found and approached: to wit, among the wiser expounders of the excellent fictions of those auncient Fathers and masters of learning and wisdome.

Liriope

L Iriope (*faire Nymphe , of* Thetis *borne*)
 The god Cephiſſus *lou'd ; and hauing long*
In vaine her maidenly denialls boarne,
Forc'd her at laſt his ſiluer ſtreames among.
'Tweene them a buoye was got, faire as the Morne,
And (if truth were in graue Tireſia's *toung)*
Immortall as his Sire; might be know neuer,
But liue a ſtranger to himſelfe for euer.

No ſooner from his birth-day had the Sun
After three Luſters, in his carre of light
Three yearely rounds more through the Zodiack run,
When this bright-viſadg'd buoye (Narciſſus *hight)*
Was growne to that ſupreme perfection
Of beauty' and grace, combinde to breed delight,
As no degree, no ſexe, no age are free ,
But all perforce of him enamour'd be.

The winning features of his face were ſuch ,
As the beſt beauties ſeem'd to his, but bad ;
Sweet, ſoft, and freſh to looke vpon, and touch,
The tender hue was of the louely lad ;
Widdowes deſir'd, and married wiues as much ,
And eu'ry maid a longing for him had ;
No harte ſo chaſte, and free from amo'rous fire ,
But he could tainte, and kindle with deſire.

Yet

Yet his proude hawty minde had in diſdaine
What euer beauty came within his ſight;
Nor car'de the choyceſt Virgins loue to gaine,
Whereto by kinde, Nature doth man inuite;
Nor yet of riper women ſought to' obtaine
The vs'de allay of the blouds appetite;
But only lou'de, ador'de, and deiſi'de
Himſelfe, diſpizing all the worlde beſide.

One day, that louely browe, thoſe liuely eyes,
That ruby lip, that alabaſter chinne
And crimſon cheeke of his, a Nymphe eſpyes,
A Nymphe that neuer doth to ſpeake beginne,
But readily to ſuch as ſpeake, replies;
Though all her words lame and imperfeſt been,
While in her mouthe confounding all the reſt,
Her laſt worde only comes out perfeſteſt.

This Nymphe which then, and ſtill we Eccho name,
That anſwers others ſpeeche, but ſpeakes to none,
Was not as now, a meere voice peec'd, and lame,
But forme and ſubſtance had of fleſh and bone;
When to her toung that imperfeſtion came
To vente but halfe wordes, and them not her owne,
Through a diſdaine ſhee in the breſte did raiſe
Of Iuno, ieliow of her huſbands wayes.

Ere

Ere which a voyce ſhee had, ſo ſweete to th' eare,
With a diſcourſe ſo ſmooth, and full of pleaſure,
As it a heauen was her wordes to heare ,
Wordes which the heauyeſt grieuance and diſpleaſure
Could mitigate, and eaſyer make to beare,
(Of ſweete and ſage ſo equall was their meaſure;)
For ſtill ſhee kept them by diſcretion good,
Within the ſeemely bounds of womanhood.

Farre was this faire maydes faire toungs glory ſpred,
Winning the minds of all men, by the ſwaye
Of her imperious eloquution ledd,
Wherewith a thouſand brabbles euery daye
Among the Nymphes, Siluans, and ſhepherds bredd
Shee eaſily atton'de; but Heau'ns queene (aye
Frying in a jelious fire) refte her of the' honour   [her.
Of her ſmooth ſpeech, for the ſhrewd turnes 't had done

Iuno, that euer had a ielious head,
(Her huſband did ſo ofte her bed abuſe)
Meaning t'haue ſtolne vpon him, where i'bed
Shee thought he tooke the pleaſure he did vſe,
This Nymphe to' auuerte (by good aduizement ledd)
The miſchiefe that ſuch errors ofte enſues,
Would with ſmooth ſtoryes entertayne his queene,
Till he had time to get away vnſeene.

N

Hauing

Hauing bin oft beguild with this deceipt,
Iuno at length th' ayme of her ſpeech perceiu'd,
And ſayd, You ſhall (Nymphe) with your ſuttle bayte
Catch me no more, or I am much deceiu'd;
Your fluent toung ſhall haue a medcine ſtraite,
That by it I may be neuer after grieu'd;
When you haue fewer words to ſpeake, wee'll ſee
How you can make your wonted ſporte with me.

And what ſhe threatned, quickly tooke effect;
For, from that time ſhe could ſpeake plaine no more,
Nor but repeate (ſuch was her toungs defect)
Peeces of words that had bin ſpoke before.
This Nymphe, the buoy whom ſo much beauty deckt
No ſooner view'd, but loue aſſayled ſore
Her breſt; ſhe prooues to him her thoughts to breake
In words, but cannot firſt begin to ſpeake.

Amaz'd as mute ſhe ſtands, loth to be ſeene,
And to a thicket by, anon ſhe hyes;
Thence, (where he layd was on a flowry greene,)
Conuayes about him her attentiue eyes
In many a fearefull glance, the boughs betweene,
Then, how to' aproach him neerer, doth deuize;
Still with new fuell feeding her deſire,
Till all her breſt falls of a burning fire.

                                        while

While thus th' inkindled maide ⁓viewes him ⁓unſeene,
And neither yet, a word to other ſpake,
He heares a noiſe among the buſhes greene
That ⁓unawares her foote did (tripping) make,
And lookes if any had about him been,
But ſees not her that languiſht for his ſake.
Heare I not one ? quoth he ; One , ſayes the mayde :
Framing a troth from the laſt word he ſayd.

Much at this voyce began the lad to muze ,
But whence it yſſue'd could not yet deuize ;
And as men oft on ſuch occaſion vſe ,
Now heere now there he throwes his earneſt eyes ;
Then once againe he thus his ſpeech renewes ,
May not I ſee thee ? ſhe, I ſee thee, cryes ;
He turnes, and looks this way, and that againe ;
She feares and hides her, and he looks in ⁓vaine.

Still more and more amaz'd he growes, and goes
Searching each place about him buſily ,
But nothing finds : then cryes come hither ; thoſe
Words ſhe returnes, and cryes come hither ; he
Sayes heere I am, do thou thy ſelfe diſcloſe,
For as I heare, faine would I know thee. She
Replyes I know thee : ſo ſhe did ; for none
Ere came ſo neere her harte as he had done.

He

He addes (deſirous to heare out the reſt)
If then thou know'ſt me , come and let's imbrace ;
And let's imbrace, ſhee ſoone replyes : that bleſt
And ſoueraigne worde inforc'd her from the place
Where ſhe was hidd, and from her mayden breſt
Chaſing her feare , ſhe appeares before the face
Of the faire buoy, whoſe words aſſur'd her cleerely ,
She ſhould imbrace him whom ſhe lou'd ſo dearely.

Her neck to wreathe with his, ſhe faire enclin'd,
Her armes to meete his armes, extended be ;
But he that was quite of another minde,
Sayes, Do not thinke I loue thee ; readily
I loue thee, ſhe replyes. rudely vnkinde
He addes, nor euer will I loue thee. She
Still ſayes, I loue thee , as ſhe ſaid before ;
He held his peace, and ſhe could ſpeake no more.

She hides her ſhaming eyes. the froward lad
Puſheth her from him , and then from her flies.
She ynly raues, well nigh with ſorrow mad
To haue woo'd him ſo, that doth her loue deſpize ;
And if by ſuch a toung as erſt ſhe had ,
But halfe the griefe that in her boſome lyes
Were vtt'red, ſhe might mooue with her laments
The heau'ns, the Earth , and all the Elements.

Her

Her pale ſick lookes the woefull witneſſe beare
Of her hartes agonye, and bitter teene;
Her fleſh ſhe batters, martyrs her faire haire,
And , ſhaming ere to be of any ſeene,
Hides her in ſome wilde wood or caue , and there
Anſwers perhaps if ſhe haue queſtion'd been;
And more and more increaſeth eu'ry day
Loues flame in her, and meltes her life away.

That flame eftſoone gan all her body blaſt;
Th'humor and bloud reſolu'd into groſſe aire;
The fleſh to aſhes in a moment paſt,
That was ſo ſleeke to feele, and look'd ſo faire,
The bones and voice only remain'd at laſt;
But ſoone the bones to hard ſtones turned are;
All that of her now liues is th'empty ſound
That from the caues doth to our eares rebound.

Beſide this Nymphe, not the moſt faire Napæa
Or Hamadriad *that was euer borne ,*
Could mooue Narciſſus; *no not* Cytherea
Or wiſe Minerua *could his fancy turne.*
Mong the neglected troope, a Nymphe to' Aſtræa
For iuſtice prayes, and vengiance on the ſcorne
Of this diſdainefull youth, that doth deſpize
Not nymphes alone, but heau'nly deities.

                       O thou

O thou (ſhe cryes) whoſe all-impartiall hand
The balance of heau'ns Equity ſuſtaines,
Do on this hawty head that doth withſtand
Nature , and heau'n, and all the world diſdaines,
Due juſtice; ô let ſome auengeing brande
Teach him by 's owne to pitty others paines,
And graunt he may himſelfe approoue the grieues
He hath to thouſands giu'n , and daily giues.

The juſt Petition that this Nymphe prefer'd,
Which ſhe with rayning eyes repeated oft,
The Poures immortall had no ſooner heard,
But they Ramnuſia ſummond from alofte,
Whoſe ſad doome was (and was not long defer'd)
That loue ſhould render his hard booſome ſoft ;
But ſuch a loue , and of ſo ſtrange a nature,
As nere before poſſeſſed human creature.

Within a ſhady groue (vnder a hill)
That opes into a medow faire, and wide,
Whoſe ample face a thouſand py'ed floures fill ,
And many' an odorous herbe, and plant beſide ,
Riżeth a fountaine freſh and coole ; for ſtill
The wood of one, and of the other ſide
The ſhady ſhoulders, of the hill defende it,
That the warme midday ſun cannot offende it.

The

The water of this well is euer cleare,
And of that wonderfull tranſparency,
That his deepe bottome ſeemes to riſe, and neere
Offer it ſelfe to the behoulders eye.
The hot Sun burnes the ground, and eu'ry where
Shepherd and ſheep to the coole ſhadowes fly;
When loue, (to' auenge him ſelfe) to this Fount guideth
This louely buoy in whom no loue abideth.

Scalt with the Sun, and weary with the chace,
He ſeekes to reſt himſelfe, and quench his thirſt,
And glad of hauing found ſo fit a place,
Layes by his bow and quiuer from him firſt,
Then, his impatient drouth away to chace,
Inclines him to the flattring Fount. accurſt
For euer may that trech'erous mirhor be
Wherin he hapt his own faire ſhade to ſee.

While ore the Fountaines face his faire face lyes,
And greedy lips the cooling liquor draw,
A greater heate doth in his breſt ariſe,
Caus'd by tke ſhade he in the water ſaw.
Loue finding ſoone whereon he fixt his eyes,
Gan to the head his goulden arrow draw,
And all his hart with the vaine loue infeſted
Of what the liquid-chriſtall glaſſe refleſted.

The

The beautious image that he ſees ſo cleerely,
And his owne ſhadow in the fountaine makes ;
Not for a ſhadow immateriall meerely,
But for a body palpable, he takes;
Each part apart, then altogether neerely
Viewes, and growes thirſtier as his thirſt he ſlakes ;
His eye his owne eye ſees, and loues the ſight ,
While with it ſelfe it doth it ſelfe delight.

He' extolls the lip, admires the cheeke, where he
The red and white ſo aptly mingled findes ;
His either eye a ſtarre he deemes to be ;
The ſhining haire that the brow faire imbindes,
He calls a ſun-beame,'tis ſo bright to ſee ;
And his affection ſo his reaſon blindes,
As all this faire for which all eyes adore him,
He ſtill imputes to what he ſees before him.

Long gazing with this earneſt admiration,
(Which well his eu'ry geſture teſtifies,)
The ſhadow ſeemes copartner in his paſſion,
And in the ſame unreſt to ſympathize ;
His owne each motion in the ſelfe ſame faſhon
Appearing manifeſtly to his eyes ;
The ſame expreſſion that he giues his paine ,
The ſame the ſhadow renders him againe.

The ſame

Tranſported with the ſilly vaine deſire
That the deceiptfull ſhadow breedes in him,
With his inkindled lips he preſſes nigher
To kiſſe the lips that on the water ſwimme ;
Thoſe lips, as if they did his lips require,
Ariʒe with equall haſt to the wells brimme ;
But his abuſed lips their purpoſe miſſe,
And only the deluding water kiſſe.

The water (troubled) doth the ſhade deface
With many’ a wrinkle, he for feare to looʒe it,
Extends with louing haſt ouer the place
His greedy armes, of either ſide to’ incloʒe it;
But they (beguild) only vaine ayre imbrace ;
He frowing lookes againe;that frownes; he wooes it
Againe with ſmiles. ah dire and cruell law
Of thy owne frowne (poore buoy) to ſtand in awe.

Yll-fated wretch, alas what doſt thou ſee
That in thy breſt this mutiny awakes ?
Perceiu’ſt thou not that what enamors thee
Is but the ſhadow thy owne body makes ?
And of how ſtrange , and ſilly’ a quality
The paſſion is wherewith thy boſome akes,
That fondly flatters thee,’tis ſtill without thee,
When what thou ſeek’ſt, thou euer bear’ſt about thee?

O   So

So neere about thee , as thou needſt not feare
But while thou tarrieſt heere , 'twill tarry too;
And when thou weary art of ſtaying heere ,
'Twill go along with thee where ere thou goe :
I ſee thine eyes blubbred with many'a teare,
And weary'ed , yet not ſatisfy'd with woe ;
Thou mourn'dſt at firſt , to' allay and eaſe thy paine,
And now thon mourn'ſt to ſee that mourne againe.

The teares the ſhadow ſhedds, doth this accurſt
Fonde louer for a firme aſſurance take,
That what he loues, feeles no leſſe amorous thirſte ,
And in compaſſion ſorrowes for his ſake.
He opes his armes to' imbrace it at firſt ;
The Shade conſents, and doth like geſture make :
He nothing gripes ; but turnes , and rudely teares
His haire, and drownes his roſy cheekes in teares.

Deſire of food , nor want of ſleepe can free
His thought from proſequuting ſtill the woe
His tirannizing Paſſion breedes , whence he
Becoms a deſpe'rate praye to his lou'd foe ;
Th' enamourd eyes will nere auuerted be
From their owne ſplendor, that enthralls him ſo ,
As (ſpight of any reaſon can inſtruct him)
They ſure will to a ſpeedy death conduct him.

He

He riſes up at length, and ſtanding by,
Pointes to the Founte, as author of the wrong
His hart receiu'd through his unwary eye;
Then theſe ſad accents the leau'd woods among
Sighes from his breſts impatient agony;
Yee woods to whome theſe wailing words belong,
(For you alredy haue beheld in parte
The wretched plight of my afflicted harte.)

Yee woods, whoſe browes to heau'n, and feete to hell
Through th' ayre and ample earth extended be,
That haue ſo long held your faire right ſo well
Againſt th' unciuile winters injury,
And many' a loue-ſick wight haue ſure heard tell
The ſtory of his ſadd captiuity
'Mong your dumb ſhades, O tell mee' if euer breſt
Y' haue heard with ſuch a loue as mine, poſſeſt.

What harte ere ſuch a darkneſſe found to' infould it,
To loue a falſe and fleeting thing ſo deare,
Which when I thinke within my armes I hould it,
Is fled from me, and I am nere the neere;
I finde my error; ſomewhat does withhould it,
And my deluſion plainely doth appeare;
Yet can I nere the more auuerte my minde
From ſeeking ſtill what I ſhall neuer finde.

O 2

But

But ſee this woe that doth all woe ſurmount,
What is it barres, what is it hinders me?
Is't either foming ſea, or craggy mount,
Strong gate, or thick wall rear'd to' eternity?
Alas'tis but a narrow ſhallow fount
That's interpos'd tweene my deſires and me,
Where what I ſeeke, appeares, & would come to me,
Did not the jelious waters bould it fro' me.

For I my head no ſooner downwards hould,
With will to' impreſſe thoſe ruby lips with mine,
But with like will (redyer then can be tould)
It ſmiles, and doth the beautious head encline.
O thou faire fabrick of celeſtiall mould
Come forth, and let our lips and boſomes joine;
Leaue that vnfriendly fountaine, and come hether,
And ſporte me in this flowry mede together.

Aymee I call, but none will anſwer me.
Come yet at laſt, if but to let me know
Since I am young, louely, and faire to ſee,
Why thou doſt hide thy ſelfe, and ſhunne me ſo;
Looke in my face, and view the harmony
The various floures make that there freſhly grow,
And tell me then, wherfore thou doſt abhorre
That, that a thouſand hartes do languiſh for.

                           I know

I know (wretch that I am) I know thee now :
Th' art my owne ſhadow meerely ; 'tis the ſhine
That falls vpon the waters chriſtall brow
From this bright face, and beautious limbs of mine ,
And nothing elſe ; I finde, alas I know
'Tis I and only I for which I pine ;
At my owne eyes alone (vnhappy elfe)
I light the fire wherein I burne my ſelfe.

I know that I am it, and it is I
That both the loued am , and louer too ;
But to allay my feau'rous malady
Alas what ſhall I ſay , what ſhall I doe ?
Shall I my ſelfe, to wooe my ſelfe, apply ,
Or ſtay perhaps till other do mee wooe ?
Aymee , wealth makes mee poore ; accurſed bleſſing
To pine in want, with ouer-much poſſeſſing.

Ah could I this fleſh-frame aſunder parte
And take a body from this body free ;
And (hauing what I loue ſo well, aparte,)
Deuide my loue betweene them equally,
So as they both, one interlouing harte
Poſſeſt ; I might perhaps contented be :
But ô alas it neuer may be done
To make that two, that Nature made but one.

Vnder the combrous weight my ſoule doth beare ,
Wanting the meane it ſelfe to ſatisfy ,
I fainte, and feele my death aproaching neere ;
And more I grieue a thouſand fold to dye ,
That in my ruine, that that is more deare
Then life to mee, muſt fall as well as I ;
Deaths face were not ſo ſoure to looke vpon ,
Might that ſweete face ſuruiue when I were gone.

He weepes, and to the water turnes againe ,
Where he the weeping fain'd Narciſſus *viewes ;*
And eu'ry teare which the falſe faire eyes raine,
Th' impatience of his balefull woe renewes ;
He ſtriues to touch the lou'd cauſe of his paine ,
Troubling the waters that his eyes abuſe ;
Then chafes, and cryes if I may neither feele
Nor heare, at leaſt let mee behould thee ſtill.

He raues impatient of his harts vnreſte,
His garment teares, martyrs his haire and rendes it ,
Then with his each bent fiſt, his inn'ocent breſt
Beats, but the weede he weares ſomewhat defends it ;
He findes it , and (himſelfe more to moleſte)
Remooues the garment, and ſtarknak'd offends it
With many' a churliſh blow , and ſo betakes him
Wholly to 's woe, as one whoſe ſence forſakes him.

The

The battr'ed juory breſt ſhewes to the view
Like halfe-ripe grapes, apples, halfe red, or roſes
Strew'd on ſome lilly banke, that (blowing nue)
The virgin-leaues to the warme Sun diſclozes;
And ſuch, as though chang'd from the former hue,
Yet nought at all of his firſt beauty loozes,
But ſeemes (though ſore perhaps, and akeing more)
As faire, or fairer then it was before.

He ſtoopes againe to take an other ſight
Of the belou'd occaſion of his woe;
The water ſhewes him ſoone the euill plight
The fleſh was in had boarne ſo many' a blow;
He mournes to ſee't; and ſtody'ing how he might
Heale, and appeaze what he had iniur'd ſo,
His armes (though well he knowes the labour vaine)
He needes will plunge into the fount againe.

The water mooues, he mournes, the Shadow flyes;
He lets it ſettle, and then lookes againe.
And now the fatall fire wherein he fryes,
His Sence conſumes, through too much ſence of paine;
So th'ore, that in a melting furnace lyes,
Growes warme, then hot; nor long doth ſo remaine,
But meltes, (the fire tyring vpon't the whiles)
And fuſible,' as the liquid water boiles.

The

The white, and faire vermilion faded be
That late imbelliſht and adorn'd him ſo;
His eye the faint lidd couers heauily;   [though
Each limbe growes ſlack and powreleſſe. Ecco al-
He loath'd and vs'd her ſo diſdainefully
Hath ſtill accompany'de him in his woe,
And euer would repeate, and anſwer make
Well as ſhe could, to whatſoere he ſpake.

What ſound his hands (beating each other) made,
Or when his boſome felt their battery,
She the like ſound returnes. he to the Shade
Languiſhing cryes, Behould for thee I dye:
For thee I dye, anſwers th'inamour'd maide,
Remembring her owne cruell deſtiny.
At length he ſadly ſighes farwell, and dyes.
Farewell ſayes Eccho, and no more replyes.

His ghoſt is to the ſhades infernall gon,
And (carry'ng ſtill his error with him) there
Lookes him in thoſe pale ſtreames of Acheron,
And wooes, & winnes himſelfe, and ne're the neere.
The Nymphes and hamadryads eu'ry one
With the ſad Nayads whc his ſiſters were,
With ſhriekes & cryes which they to heau'n inforce,
Strew their faire ſhorne haires on the bloudleſſe corſe.
                                        Ecco

Ecco, (that grieues no leſſe then th'other do)
Confounds her lamentation lowd with theirs;
And would her treſſes teare, and her fleſh too,
Had ſhe them ſtill; but as ſhe may, ſhe beares
Her part in eu'ry ſound of griefe, and woe,
That from beat hand, or wayling voice ſhe heares.
If any (weeping) cry, aymee he's gone,
She ſayes the ſame, and multiplies the moane.

His fun'erall pile rounded with tapers bright,
The wayling Nymphes prepare without delay;
But the dead corſe is vaniſht from their ſight;
And in the place where the pale carcaſſe lay,
A flowre with yellow ſeed, and leaues milke white
Appeares; a fairer flowre Aprill nor May
Yeelds; for it keeps much of his beauty ſtill.
Some call't a Lilly, ſome a Daffadill.

Obſeruation vpon the Tale of Marciſſus.

As not the leaſt of the Fables of
the Auncients but had their mea-
P   nings,

nings, and moſt of them diuerſe meanings alſo, ſo no leſſe hath this of
Narciſſus, which *Ouid* hath ſmoothe-
ly ſung, and I paraphraſtically Eng-
gliſht after my owne way, and for
my owne pleaſure. Wherein I am
not vnwilling to render (withall)
what, as I am taught a little by my
owne *Genius*, and more by better vn-
derſtandings then my own, the Fable
was by the firſt deuizers therof made
to meane. And firſt, for the Geo-
the Geogra- graphick parte; the Sence thereof is
phick ſence. (I conceiue) obuious enough : The
Tale tells vs, the god *Cephiſſus*, a great
Riuer in *Bœotia*, that running through
the *ager Atticus* or *Attick* field (as the
place was aunciently called) meetes,
and mingles his ſtreames with the
Water-nymphe *Liriope*, a narrow
brooke ſo named, and hauing betweene them compaſſed a flat low
ground almoſt Iland-wiſe, before
their

their falling together into the *Phale-rick* gulphe , they were fitly called the Parents of this *Narciſſus* or *Daffa-dill* , beeing a floure which , (befides the fpecificall nature it hath to grow, and thriue beſt in waterifh places ,) the medowy groundes thofe waters encompaſſed , did chiefely yeeld and abound in. This *Narciſſus* is fai-ned to efchew and flye the compa-nie of all women, no leſſe then of the Nymphe *Ecco* that is enamour'd and doates vpon him ; denoting by this auuerfion of his, the nature of the floure that beares his name ; for the *daffadill* or *water-lilly* , the feedes thereof efpecially (as the applyers of them in medcine haue obferued) do powerfully extinguifh the ability and defire of carnall copulation , by ouercooling of the animall feed ; no leſſe then does Porcelane, Lettuce, *Agnus caſtus* , Calamint , White vio-

the Phyſick ſence.

letts

P 2

letts, and the like of that kinde. From this his before mencioned quality, and the ill effect it workes in mans body, his name *Narciffus* (which is *torpedo, languor, fegnities*-flothe, ftupiditie, lazineffe) was by the Auncients not vnfitly giuen to this vegitable. And they out of this confideration likewife faigned that *Proferpine*, when *Pluto* rauifhed her away as fhe was gathering floures, had her lap full of *Narciffuffes*; becaufe lazy & vnbufied women are moft fubject vnto fuch inconueniences. And becaufe flothfull, vnactiue, and vninduftrious mindes are for the moft parte vncapable of producing any permanent, fubftantiall or reall effects or frute in any kinde, this fraile flowre therefore (the fymbole of fuch like imperfect and dificient inclinations,) was among the number of loft , dead , and foone-to-be-forgotten things, by

thofe

thofe Auncient inueftigators of Natures trueths , particularly dedicated
to their Infernall gods. The Morall
expounders of this Fable will haue
it meane thus,-*Ecco*, or Fame, (a faire
voice) loues and wooes *Narciffus* , or
Philautia ; but the felfe-louing man ,
enamor'd (like this *Narciffus*) only
on himfelfe , and blinde to all plea-
fures but thofe of the Sence, defpifes
and flightes the more to be imbraced
happineffe of a lafting renowne , and
memory ; and therefore dying , his
fame , and all of him dyes with him ,
and he becomes only-*charus dis inferis.*
A much higher and nobler meaning
then any of thefe before deliuered , is
by excellent Authors giuen to this
Fable : wherein we muft know,that
as all the firft wife Auncients in generall, vnder characters, figures, and
fimboles of things, layd downe the
precepts of their wifdome to Pofterity,

the Morall fence.

the Diuine fence.

rity , fo in particular did *Pythagoras*,
who (as the moſt autentick *Iamblicus*
the *Caldæan* tells vs) deliuered alſo
the moſt parte of his doctrines in fi-
guratiue, tipick, and ſymbolick Notions: among which , one of his documents is this-*While the winds breathe,
adore Ecco.* This *Winde* is (as the be-
fore-mencioned *Iamblicus*, by conſent
of his other fellow-*Cabaliſts* ſayes) the
Symbole of the Breath of God ; and
Ecco, the Reflection of this diuine
breath, or Spirit vpon vs ; or (as they
interpret it)-*the daughter of the diuine
voice ;* which through the beatifying
ſplendor it ſhedds & diffuſes through
the Soule , is juſtly worthy to be re-
uerenced and adored by vs. This *Ecco*
deſcending vpon a *Narciſſus* , or ſuch
a Soule as (impurely and vitiouſly
affected) ſlights , and ſtops his eares
to the Diuine voice , or ſhutts his
harte frō diuine Inſpirations,through
his

his being enamour'd of not himſelfe,
but his owne ſhadow meerely, and
(buried in the ordures of the Sence)
followes corporall ſhadowes, and
flyes the light and purity of Intellectuall Beauty, he becoms thence (being diſpoyled, (as the great *Iamblicus*
ſpeakes) of his propper, natiue, and
celeſtiall vertue, and ability,) an ear-
thy, weake, worthleſſe thing, and
fit ſacrifize for only eternall obliui-
on, and the *dij inferi*; to whom the
Auncients (as is before noted) be-
queathed and dedicated this their lazy, ſtupid, and for-euer-fameleſſe
Narciſſus.

F ʒ N ʒ S,

Errata.

FOl: 2. lin: 7. for than. read then, and so throughout the booke.

fol: 3. lin: 12. for hotheaded reade hot-headed.

foi: 10. lin: 13. for it it hath r. it hath.

fol: 21. lin: 7. for integer, r. integer. in the marginall note ibid for *Bavoaldus* r. *Beroaldus*, and for write his praises. 1 r. with his praises.

fo: 22. lin: 20. for. and and graces. r. and graces.

fo: 23. lin: 12. for whither r. whether.

fo: 24. lin: vltim: for. are held in the. Poet espetially. r. are held in. the Poet espetially.

fo: 26. lin: 7. for prefession r. profession. and 5. lines after for fawning r. fawnings.

ibid: lin: 22. for *publicam*. r. *pudicam.*

fo: 31. lin: 4. for. *Homer* likewise. r. In *Homer* likewise.

fo: 33. lin: 20. for. a hauebin as. r. as haue bin a.

fo: 36. lin. 2. for than. r. then.

fo: 40. lin. vltim: for *Rabi Moyses.* r. *Rabi Moysis.*

fo: 43. lin: 4. for kuowledge. r. knowledge.

fo: 55. lin. 11. for of them; made. r. of them) made.

fo: 61. lin: 1. for. dignies. r. dignities.